MW00354466

Connectedness: Leadership for a Changing World

CONNECTEDNESS

Katrin Winkler & Nicola Bramwell

LEADERSHIP FOR A CHANGING WORLD

Linchpin Books

Illustrations by Richard Lidbetter
Cover image courtesy of PantherMedia
Book layout and cover by Jurgen Leemans

ISBN 9789464075403
D/2020/15004/01

© The Bayard Holding bv – publishing house Linchpin Books, 2020

All rights reserved. No part of this publication may be reproduced,
stored in a retrieval system, or transmitted in any form or by any means, electronic,
mechanical, photocopying, recording, scanning or otherwise, except as permitted by law,
without either the prior written permission of the author and the publisher.

Linchpin Books is a trade name of The Bayard Holding bv, Registered in Belgium, No. BE 0629 734 985
www.linchpinbooks.eu

Foreword
by Peer M. Schatz

Figure 1: **Peer M. Schatz**

When asked what I consider the most critical element of business success, my one piece of advice to any leader is to build a team of people who have trust in each other and who genuinely understand and believe in your mission.

I have seen so many organizations with fantastic strategies and great products fail to deliver on their potential simply due to lack of trust, conviction and focus on what's not possible versus what is possible. However, whenever an organization prioritizes the reason why they exist and makes it very clear how every member of the team can achieve professional and personal fulfilment by pursuing this mission, the success rate goes up tremendously.

An environment where everyone knows how they can make a difference and where people share the desire to do so will be an open environment in which information and ideas move quickly and where strategic and organizational agility will create a competitive advantage and stimulate trust, initiative and ensure a shared ownership of the organization's mission. These are typically also environments where senior management leads by example, is visible yet also humble and also recognizes contributions.

Of course, success also requires a great deal of hard work, ideas, processes and good fortune, yet when these above factors come together, we can often see significant increases in success which is then also achieved in an inclusive and inspiring way. Such success is also often more sustainable as it reinforces a culture which can create a source of long-lasting energy. For most of my professional career, I had the great privilege to be part of organizations that have embraced the principles of transformational leadership and I have seen for myself the impact such leaders can have.

As a leader, I have always seen it as the most gratifying experience to be able to work alongside truly engaged and engaging people, who share a passion for a shared mission and thereby unleash a tremendous, positive energy – and not only deliver business results but thereby experience and share personal fulfilment which is often evidenced by a working atmosphere in which, even when great challenges are being faced, one can experience joy, laughter and a great can-do spirit. That is where true magic happens.

Peer M. Schatz

Peer M. Schatz is long-time Chief Executive Officer of QIAGEN N.V., a leading provider of molecular sample and assay technologies. Between 1993 to 2019, he led QIAGEN's rapid expansion from a start up with $2 million in sales into a global leader with over $1.6 billion in revenues. Mr. Schatz also served as a founding member of the German Corporate Governance Commission and served as a director or advisory board member of several publicly listed companies as well as of the Frankfurt Stock Exchange. Mr Schatz graduated from the University of St. Gallen, Switzerland with a Master's Degree in Finance and from the University of Chicago Graduate School of Business as a Master of Business Administration.

Authors

Figure 2: **Dr Katrin Winkler**

Professor Dr Katrin Winkler is a Human Resources and Leadership professor at the University of Applied Sciences (UAS) Kempten, Germany. As both academic professor and having many years' experience leading international teams and consulting for leaders around the world, she shares her insights on effective leadership and how to motivate and inspire people.

Figure 3: **Nicola Bramwell**

Nicola Bramwell has an MBA and business background in strategic marketing, general management, human resource management, organizational design and leadership. She has held senior positions in blue chip companies in complex industries and shares much expertise in innovative leadership, leading change, and developing effective communication skills and personal impact.

Contents

Introduction
Achieving Balance

Our Passion for Leadership

Leadership is about stepping forward, inspiring and motivating others to get involved and creating an environment in which all can succeed. So, what's new? In the 21st century, challenges are global such as climate change, pandemics, economic pressure, education, integration and keeping pace with technology (1). These are rapid changes. For business, such changes, driving a new knowledge era, rather than the industrial focus of the 20th century, means business organizations also need a rethink. They need less bureaucracy, more innovation, more flexibility. This also impacts business leaders and a refocus on leadership that can unleash the energy and talent to make all this all happen (2). One other significant trend in this century, as described succinctly by the Dalai Lama, is fostering a oneness, through dialogue and respect (3). This theme of oneness or connectedness is what this book reflects most. It is allowing businesses to make improvements in life, whilst using purpose, the connectedness to something bigger than ourselves, to achieve extraordinary things. For leaders, be they senior managers, project managers or those simply influencing as role models, this means being true to one's self and connecting with others.

For successful leadership today we believe the work still has to be done, tasks completed, goals achieved, and financial results secured. What we also believe and have evidence to show, is that greater success, even happiness, can be found by shifting focus, by going beyond task orientation to people orientation. In other words, beyond traditional management and control, to true leadership. It requires a mind shift though, and a deep personal shift from ego and ambition to purpose and connectedness (4). Sounds unreal? We don't believe so and here we will show you why and how!

This book is designed as an inspiring "management book" which covers the key concepts managers and leaders need to know: from what businesses need to manage, to the importance of people management, through to how to lead people. It does however consider how to do these things *and* fulfil the human need for personal growth, finding our calling and gaining a sense of belonging. The book therefore references much from management and leadership experts, as well as challenging many Western norms and considering topics related to virtues and values. It is designed to make you think, possibly question established habits and inspire individuals to take a moment and redefine how they truly make a difference every single day.

New Business Approach

"Today's corporate environments are leaner. Priority is value-creation from every contributor and in every interaction. The traditional, hierarchical notion of leadership no longer serves the needs of the organization" (5). What has also been shown, is that regardless of desire to change, organizations have only kept up the pressure and the impact on employees has worsened. The Gallup Institute has been conducting studies on employee engagement since 2001. Their constant key finding is that despite the fact that employees in general have a positive relationship towards work and most rate their surrounding conditions positively, including work-life balance or compensation, strong employee engagement can only be found within 15% of an organization (6). 70% of employees are basically just doing what they are told to do and show no extra effort. And 15% are entirely disengaged and so utterly frustrated that they actually start to sabotage the organization!

Yet people really want to contribute and are motivated when starting a job, and it is the leadership behaviours that often lead to disengagement (7) or in the worst-case situation, to people starting to turn against the company.

This leads us to again highlight that there has to be a better way! We spend so much of our lives at work so how can we make this more fulfilling and the type of place where people want to give the best of themselves every day? It has been shown that "employees don't just want to work for a company, they want to belong to an organization" (8). So, how can we engage people's minds and nourish their souls? It is simply about doing the right things for the organization *and* doing them in the right way for people.

The new way is all about balance:
- Effective management focus and leadership trust
- Balancing tasks and people orientation
- Handling complexity through flexibility
- Going beyond controlling people to including people
- And it's greater than outdated or imagined orders; it is about emotional connectedness and purpose.

This book concentrates on the opportunities for leading in a new way. Imagine the outcomes when teams are: connected by a shared purpose and led by courage, kindness and curiosity; highly engaged with organizational vision and values; motivated to contribute and achieve organizational success. By understanding that the new world requires a new way of leading can open the door for the creation of **transformational environments**: a shift to purpose and values underpinned by strong management and leadership. What we want to share is how leaders can go about doing this.

The Transformational Environment

A transformational environment can be created when applying connectedness in the digital age: connecting with self, others and the business, to achieve fulfilment as individuals, teams and organizations.

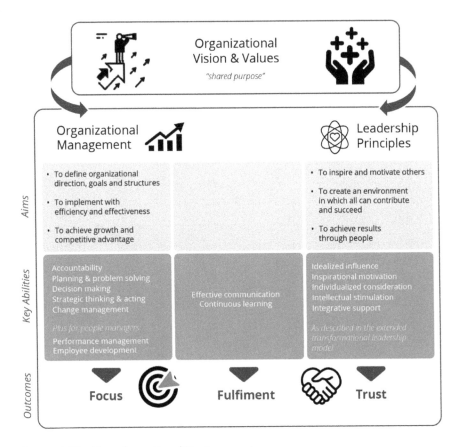

Figure 4: The Transformational Environment

Why Leadership and Connectedness Count Today

Welcome to Part One, our introduction to leadership today. From understanding the management and leadership tasks that need to take place, to understanding what is changing around us, we explore the complexities and challenges for successful leadership, which we believe lie not in isolationism, but in leveraging all connections around us.

Chapter 1
Global Companies Need Management and Leadership

Key Knowledge...

- Management is a process of directing a team to achieve planned objectives
- Leadership is achieving results through people
- Leaders are measured by actions, not position

Key Actions...

- Managing includes planning, strategy and setting objectives; organizing time, work and decision making; controlling, correcting errors and appraising performance; and achieving tasks
- People management includes setting individual goals, team building and developing
- Leading includes translating vision into meaning for individuals, inspiring all individuals to gain commitment and creating the environment for business and individual success

Impacts...

- Alignment and accountability to business objectives, resulting in high performing organizations, teams and individuals
- Greater agility and openness to change
- Long term competitive advantage and growth

Let's start with the basics; what is management? Simply put, management is a process of directing a team to achieve planned objectives, but before we explore how to do this, let's start by considering what a business is and how a business works.

A business produces and sells goods (or provides a service) to customers. Michael Porter described the activities of a company as the value chain, which highlights the steps undertaken to create value in the eyes of a customer (9). Primary activities include raw material sourcing, production, plus sales and distribution of the final product. Supporting activities include functions related to providing infrastructure, finance and human resources.

The Value Chain

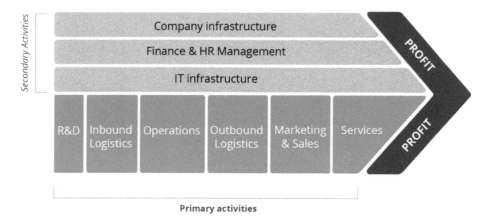

Figure 5: Representation of The Value Chain (9)

A business must also make profit, the excess the customer is willing to pay over the costs incurred to make and sell the products (or service offering in service industries). How a business is setup and run to achieve this relates to how it is managed. To create value, the senior management team of a business therefore has to understand the customers and make decisions on how to formulate the business to deliver results. Management gurus such as Drucker (10) and Malik (11) agree that it's about doing the right things and doing them in an aligned way.

Figure 6: Management Decisions

To achieve results, a business has to make a clear decision on Strategy, Structure and Culture to be able to provide orientation for the organization and drive results:

Strategy. Strategy is all about products, long term planning and how to be better and faster than the competition. The strategy of the organization defines what to focus on and thus provides orientation for the employees.

Structure. Structure defines how activities such as task allocation, coordination and supervision are directed towards the achievement of the business strategy, through teams, divisions or functional areas. It defines the set up of the organization and how the resources are allocated to deliver on the strategy.

Culture. Culture can be described as the corporate glue which creates an environment of identity and belonging for the employees. A corporate culture consists of the underlying norms and values and can be seen in the actions and behaviours of the people. Parts of corporate culture are visible, such as artefacts defined in corporate branding, yet a lot of it is not visible and consists of shared values which are not always expressed succinctly yet have a major impact on driving the behaviour of employees (12).

These three elements are translated to employees to drive their daily tasks and actions, which bring about the business results. Many companies align, implement and communicate their business approach in a highly structured way, such as a strategy pyramid.

A Strategy Pyramid

Figure 7: **Strategy Pyramid**

A strategy pyramid is a structured framework which provides orientation and the corridor for decisions in an organization. This framework can include creating and communicating:

- *A vision* – long term aims and direction
- *Mission* – the purpose of the organization
- *Values* – what the organization believes in and the principles employees are expected to uphold
- *Goals* – SMART objectives for the next 1-3 years
- *Strategies* – the plans showing how to achieve goals
- *Competencies* – success behaviours for which all employees will be assessed and developed.

Such a structured approach feeds directly into key initiatives, projects and daily tasks.

Management is a Process of Doing the Right Things

As Malik defined management (14), it is "the profession of effectiveness, with no space for failures".

It is:
- Focused on effectiveness
- Controlling tasks and people
- Setting and achieving goals
- Producing order and consistency
- Task oriented

As management is a process, a manager must therefore decide the series of actions or steps to take in order to achieve a particular end. A manager's role can then be described as knowing the company story, focusing on company strategy and goals, translating and directing this to a team to achieve planned objectives. For management to achieve order and consistency, as well as effectiveness, it is concerned with the operational, everyday tasks, including planning and budgeting, organizing and staffing, controlling and problem solving (13). Management does, by eliminating chaos and defining processes, establish the foundations for a successful business. If management encompasses a series of steps to achieve business results efficiently and effectively, the question is, how does leadership differ?

Leadership is Going Beyond Management Tasks to Achieve Results Through People

In today's business world of disruption, change, new expectations, and easy to copy product and processes, it is leadership that is required more than ever. Leadership can be considered to give the edge. How? Well, imagine if everyone in an organization is completely bought in and working at their utmost best. With such a committed and engaged workforce, the power of human capital can be leveraged to deal with the challenges of today and bring about business success.

So, where management is a process of doing the right things, leadership is about inspiring others to be engaged and committed to work and personal success. It is...

* Creating an environment in which others can succeed
* Focused on the development of vision and strategy, with scope for failure
* People oriented, seeking commitment and building collaborations
* Aiding organizations and people to deal with complexity and change
* Supporting agility, growth and sustainable competitive advantage

'Just turning up is no longer an option'

SAHAR HASHEMI, FOUNDER OF COFFEE REPUBLIC (15)

Leadership is therefore about environment, purpose and meaning. It is concerned with direction, aligning people, motivating and inspiring (13). The result of this is to achieve change and movement. This is because leading is related to actions that influence the future of an organization and its people. And it really does matter as leaders create the environment for their team, good or bad.

There is much survey data to show why people quit their jobs. In a Gallup survey from 2008, 17% stated reasons directly related to management and for other tops answers such as "career advancement" and "lack of fit to the job", the leader also has influence (16). In a more recent 2016 Gallup survey, 18% stated that during the last 12 months, they thought about quitting their jobs, because of their boss (17). This is why the conclusion still holds, that "at least 75% of the reasons for voluntary turnover can be influenced by managers" (16) And highlights that leaders can act to retain staff and go further to create a motivating and effective work environment.

Yet a business needs planning, organization and control! For a business to be successful, tasks have to be completed in the right way and in time; such as developing, selling and distributing products to their customers. So, to ensure this happens, tasks *and* people have to be managed.

The Grid developed by Blake and Mouton (18) helps to explain how tasks and people have to be managed. Though developed in the 1960's, it still a powerful insight into the balance needed by a "leader" to show concern or focus on both tasks and people.

The Leadership Grid

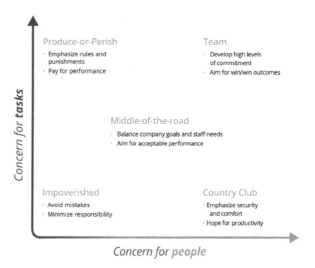

Figure 8: Representation of the Leadership Grid (18)

The grid is based on two different behavioural thoughts; concern for people, and the concern for tasks and results. Concern for people is where a leader considers the teams' needs and interests when deciding how best to accomplish a task at hand. The concern for tasks and results is where a leader points out specific objectives, readiness, and where to strengthen focus when deciding how best to accomplish the task. It also identifies five different combinations of management or leadership styles:

Impoverished leadership: The impoverished or "indifferent" leader is the most ineffective. These leaders have little to no interest to create a work environment that gets the job done. With little interest in motivating or satisfying the team, the results are almost always disorganized, lack agreement and have no satisfaction.

An example of this may be someone who is leaving or retiring. They no longer have interest in the company or the employees.

Produce-or-Perish Leadership: These types of leaders are autocratic and have strict rules, policies, and procedures. By viewing punishment as an effective way of motivating team members, this approach can lead to high results. However, this lowers the teams' morale and diminishes motivation. This will ultimately hurt people's performance. This type of leader will struggle to keep performance at a high level and no one will be happy. An example of this is if a leader takes over a department for a short period of time. They don't care for the people and just want to get the job done.

Middle-of-the-Road Leadership: A Middle-of-the-Road or "status quo" leader tries to keep a balance between results and people. This strategy sounds alright but is not as effective as it may seem. Through constant adjustments, it will not succeed in having high performances and will never fully meet the needs of the people. The result is that the team will not be very happy and that will show in the lack of productivity.

Country Club Leadership: The Country Club or "accommodating" style of leader keeps tabs on how team members are feeling. The leader assumes that as long as employees are happy and feel needed, they will work hard and perform better. An example of this is if a leader just got hired or promoted. They want to stay friendly with old peers and will forget to criticize or discipline employees.

Team Leadership: This is the most effective style and has a leader who shows passion in their work. Team leaders manage the organization's needs so that the team members understand the organizations' purpose. By involving the people in determining business needs, teams feel committed and want to have a say in how successful the organization can become. This creates a respectful environment based on trust. This will ultimately lead to higher satisfaction, more motivated employees, and overall better performance. An example of this is an experienced leader who shows commitment to their employees but does not depend on being well liked by them.

If we review the thoughts of other experts, it is clear that management and leadership are different, yet it can be argued that a business needs both.

'You manage things, you lead people'

HOPPER (19)

'Management is about coping with complexity ...
Leadership is about coping with change'

KOTTER (20)

'Where managers act to limit choices, leaders develop
fresh approaches to long-standing problems and
open issues to new options'

ZALEZNIK (21)

From Hopper (19), we can determine that managers focus on tasks, where leadership is more people oriented. John Kotter is a firm believer in innovation and change being a direct consequence of leadership, not management (20). Zaleznik also highlights that future direction and ambition comes from leadership (21). All agree therefore that management and leadership bring different things. This point is further highlighted by the rise of informal leadership in businesses today.

Leadership is Defined by Action Not Position

Though "manager" is a job, leadership is a choice. Leadership can be demonstrated in many situations as it is defined by action, not title. The challenge in business today is to understand that leadership needs to happen everywhere, meaning more people need to step forward and take the responsibility. So, if leadership is a choice, not a position, why doesn't everyone step forward?

As humans, we are subject to many unconscious biases. One is known as **bystander apathy**, a phenomenon concerning people's likeliness to help in an emergency situation. According to Bystander Apathy or the Bystander Effect, the greater the number of other people present, the less likely any one of them are to act (22). Why? There are two reasons ...when we are in a crowd, we assume that someone else will do something, and no one wants to be the person who is behaving differently. When we translate this to business, we can see the risk of dilution of responsibility in groups and secondly, the influence of social pressure that it is ok not to act when others don't. This therefore suggests that choosing to step forward to lead requires individual decision making and accountability for an outcome. For this to arise, an individual requires motivation and confidence to act.

Our intrinsic **motives** drive our actions. According to American psychologist David McClelland, we all have a need for achievement, a need for affiliation, and a need for power (23). Individuals will have different characteristics depending on their dominant motivator.

- *Achievement:* Achievement has a strong need to set and accomplish challenging goals, takes calculated risks and likes to receive regular feedback on progress and achievements.

- *Affiliation:* Affiliation wants to belong to the group, favours collaboration over competition and doesn't like high risk or uncertainty.

- *Power:* Power wants to control and influence others, win and enjoys status and recognition. Those with a strong power motivator however are often divided into two groups: personal and institutional. People with a personal power drive want to control others, while people with an institutional power drive like to organize the efforts of a team to further the company's goals.

This understanding of intrinsic motives leads us to ask if the need for power is associated with leadership? Is power and the need for power a bad thing in the workplace?

Here are some connotations of power in the workplace: It is associated with responsibility; it facilitates decision making and those deciding set the future direction. It does however create boundaries……so not bad in general, however negative connotations come from misuse of power.

'With great power comes great responsibility'

CHURCHILL, *ET AL*

'Power is a medium to arrange the decision criteria of a society and to ensure decidability'

NIKLAS LUHMANN (24)

The Significance of Power

In the 1960s, John French and Bertram Raven described five types of power in leadership (25).

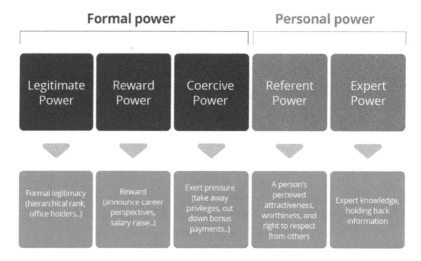

Figure 9: Representation of the Five Basis of Power (25)

Legitimate power comes from position in an organization. **Reward** also comes from the authority to make decisions on benefits to others so may be associated with compliance. **Coercive power** is pressure based and conveyed through fear such as losing your job. These three are examples of formal power.

Referent and **expert power** on the other hand are personal. *Referent power* comes from being trusted and respected for what we do and how we handle situations. *Expert power* comes from our experience, skills or knowledge and how that is also utilized by others. Both highlight that formal power is not required to lead, it is actions that count.

Understanding that influence and impact can come from outside of hierarchy is essential today due to the decline of old norms and structures in business. The days of static organizational structures with strict hierarchy, and senior managers or leaders as controllers are gone. Vertical reporting lines are being replaced by matrix structures and project teams. The idea of separation and arms-length relationships with other functions, suppliers and organizations has also gone. Upward flow of information and downward flow of decisions and directives is also a thing of the past. These remnants of a command and control structure are being replaced by leaner, flatter organizations and ones desiring contribution from all and requiring both formal and informal leadership at all levels.

The Increasing Relevance of Informal Leadership

Informal leadership is leveraging experience, knowledge, skills and the contribution of those who *choose* to step forward. It means having the ability to influence the behaviour of others, not through position and hierarchy, but based on personal referent power (trusted, respected) or expert power (as a thought leader or social influencer). Behaviours that are influenced include decision making and problem-solving, enabling more collaborative and creative approaches. This is critical for flexible project work and can directly lead to faster, more innovative and nimble organizations.

Terminology for such styles commonly expressed today can include **lateral leaders** who influence without 'title' or "position", often due to their natural inclination to get things done (5). **Agile leaders** who demonstrate the ability or agility to lead well in a wide range of circumstances especially new, changing and ambiguous situations (26). Finally, **project managers** can be included here as project management includes completion of the work of a team to achieve specific goals within a specified time, without the vertical reporting lines.

To understand informal leadership and its tasks better, let's look at examples of roles or positions within an organization.

Role Differences	Line Manager	Project Manager
Goal	• Deliver team success year on year	• Completion a defined project with a defined scope, start and finish
Responsibility	• Management of employees	• Planning and execution of a project
Tasks	• Planning, organizing, directing, controlling & reporting	• Planning, organizing, directing, controlling & reporting
Authority	• By position, rules & procedures (including organizational HR policy)	• By project board, to run the project on a day-to-day basis
Power	• Legitimate, Reward, Referent	• Expert, Referent
Leadership role	• Direct influence on team including performance management and employee development	• Informal influence on team to persuade

Figure 10: **Differences Between Line Manager and Project Manager Roles**

It can be seen that a line manager has the goal to deliver team success year on year and as such is responsible for the management of people and their tasks. A project manager on the other hand has to deliver a defined project. Often the tasks of line management and project management can be considered similar and both includes the work of others. The challenge however is that a project manager does not have responsibility to "manage" people. This means when influencing team members, a line manager already has positional authority. For a project manager, without formal authority, true leadership is required to influence and persuade a team.

So, as we define it, leadership is about inspiring others to be engaged and committed to work and personal success. It is establishing direction and aligning people through communication and team work. In other words, leaders influence results through people, and this needs to be achieved as a line manager or a project manager. This may also go some way to consider the question, can one person manage and lead? Or even, must one person manage and lead at the same time to be successful? We believe, yes. Kotter also advocates that a successful organization needs to combine both strong management and strong leadership.

'Companies should remember that strong leadership with weak management is no better, and is sometimes actually worse, than the reverse.

The real challenge is to combine strong leadership and strong management and use each to balance the other'

JOHN KOTTER (20)

Key Learning Points

- For management to achieve order and consistency, as well as effectiveness, it is concerned with the operational, everyday tasks, including planning & budgeting, organizing & staffing, controlling & problem solving. Management does, by eliminating chaos and defining processes, establish the foundations for a successful business

- Leadership is creating an environment in which others can succeed and going beyond managing tasks to achieving results through people. It is focused on the development of vision and direction and coping with change

- Leaders need to combine ability to manage with adaptability to lead

- True leadership, formal and informal, is essential throughout an organization, for agility and innovation. It is not limited to position and only defined by actions and outcomes

Personal Reflection Points

Question 1: Reflect upon your own experiences and development needs:

	Examples of how you demonstrate each point in teams or projects	How do you believe you could be even better?
Management Tasks		
• Planning, such as budgeting, organizing	•	•
• Staffing, such as goal setting, team building	•	•
• Controlling & measuring performance	•	•
• Daily decision making, problem solving	•	•
Leadership Tasks		
• Establishing direction	•	•
• Aligning people	•	•
• Motivating & inspiring	•	•

Figure 11: Reflection Exercise on Experiences and Development Needs

Question 2: **By plotting yourself on the grid below, what does it tell you and what you can learn?**

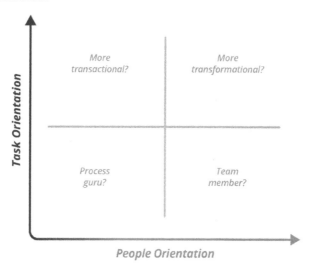

Figure 12: Reflection Exercise on The Leadership Grid

Question 3: **Would others agree with your placement above? How do you believe you are genuinely perceived by others and why?**

Chapter 2

Game Changers of Globalization and Digitalization

Key Knowledge...

- Globalization describes the growing interdependence of the world's economies, cultures, businesses and populations, due to cross-border trade and flows of investment, people, and knowledge

- Digitalization describes the restructuring of personal lives around digital communication and media infrastructure (how people interact). Digitalization also describes the use of digital technologies to change a business model, provide new revenue streams or value, producing greater business opportunities

- Both trends have changed businesses rapidly and cannot be ignored. Both can be leveraged through true leadership

Key Actions...

- Seek out new opportunities in change; see change as the norm

- Be open to new perspectives from global sources such as diverse customers and workforces

- Embrace a digital mind set to enhance all aspects of business from strategy to processes to leadership

- Identify and develop new leadership competencies

Impacts...

- Leadership innovation looks to maximise human potential, creates uniqueness, is difficult to copy and as such builds sustainable, competitive advantage

- Organizational impacts from embracing change include strategic renewal, productivity gains, less turnover, increased agility and greater brand value

- Innovative working practices impact employees resulting in better teamwork, greater company commitment, increased morale and trust

Globalization, technological innovations and other constant changes mean businesses need to be more agile and adaptable to survive. In other words, it is about embracing change as the only constant. Customer demands and expectations are rapidly evolving – they want more choice; they want goods now and they want services their way.... Competitors can be organizations from across the world – not only can they access global customers; they can recruit from a global workforce. Even the ways of working, such as more remote teams and flexible working have impacts on organizations. The jobs we do even differ from the jobs of 20 years ago. And why? Because globally, the social and economic structures have changed. All this means that businesses have to change too to stay ahead. In terms of how an organization achieves this, strong leadership is the only way to navigate through.

'If the rate of change outside exceeds the rate of change inside, the end is in sight'

JACK WELCH (27)

'Speed of change is the driving force. Leading change competently is the only answer'

JOHN KOTTER (28)

Companies in the Global and Digital Age

In the 21st century, it is the digital drive in particular that has added further complexity (29). Companies, employees and managers share common challenges of using new technologies wisely in order to achieve results and increase value. This challenge takes place in the context of disruptive societal and economic changes. In our personal lives, digitalization is the new norm, readily accessible to many and seemingly inescapable. For example, communication. By the year 2020, Cisco estimate more people will have mobile phones than electricity at home, specifically 69% of the world's population (30).

Considering companies, evidence highlights vast differences. In 2016, research showed that the degree of digitalization of German organizations for example, in comparison to companies internationally, exhibited deficiencies in the use of information and communication technologies (31). This was despite the fact that 80% of German employees used information and communication technologies (32). Why a gap? There have been two waves of digitalization (33). The first took place in the context of the third industrial revolution and manifested itself in the transfer from analogue to digital information. This wave was complete at the end of the 1990s. The second wave of digitalization, at the beginning of this century, is also the starting point of the fourth industrial revolution and primarily describes the introduction of digital processes using information and communication technologies. This process is far from complete, and going back to our German example, 38% of German companies are still at the very beginning of their digitalization efforts. Only 2% have developed and successfully implemented a digitalization strategy. Of small and medium-sized enterprises, 47% have not taken any steps (34). So, although many employees are already using information and communication technologies, companies are not yet surfing the digital wave because they have not entirely implemented digital processes. More is still to come, so which changes can we therefore expect for the business world of the future?

Digitalization leads to upheaval in all areas of structure and information flow. Modern businesses translate digitalization to mean the hyper connectivity associated with digital transformation and the end-to-end data integration of the ecosystem of a business, touching operations, customer-facing activities and connecting physical and virtual structures. Such changes set in motion highly flexible structures in organizations, as well as the virtual and network-based types of collaborative work (35).

But what does this actually mean for the design structure of the core areas of work? As a basis for investigating this question, we can look at the six structuring areas of work and consider new digitalization, as well as globalization perspectives (36).

Structuring Areas of Work

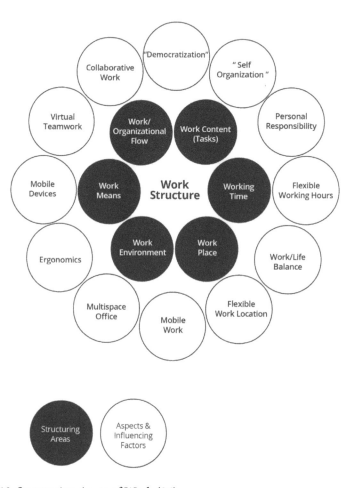

Figure 13: Structuring Areas of Work (36)

Looking at the six structuring areas in turn, changes can be readily identified due to digitalization and globalization, which in turn drive further work place modifications (36, 37).

Work flows and Organizations: Work flows and Organizations are being increasingly characterized by collaborative work in general and specifically by work in virtual teams. Jobs are created without clear organizational affiliation, for example, project teams. ***Networking*** plays a large role in this context and digital communication tools are increasingly being used for efficiency and effectiveness. A highly integrated work organization is also an absolute necessity for creating an international value-added chain. In light of such innovations, it also becomes necessary to re-think organizational structures. Thinking in fixed hierarchies must be replaced by the "democratization" of work as a focal point. This is defined by a future that has employees and managers being on par with one another and collaborating together. To achieve this, it is necessary to have an organizational culture that is characterized by allowing mistakes, promoting fairness and preventing discrimination (38). This means a clear renunciation of the practice common in many companies of evaluating productivity through working hours and therefore a change in performance management (39). Big changes in thinking!

Work Content: In a digital world, tasks are being completed through personal responsibility, which is why constant access to the work content must be ensured. Employees organize and structure their work processes by achieving results through self-organization – alone or in projects with colleagues. Due to a variety of automation solutions, routine tasks are also becoming less important and are being replaced by challenging, creative task areas, for example data entry replaced by data interpretation.

Work Means: It is obvious that key working materials for many employees are now electronic tools such as handhelds, computers and software. Managers especially are equipped with mobile devices. This results in the creation of an increased "digital aura" (40) that surrounds us and helps us to communicate and work with our environment. It also begins to stress a 24/7 culture.

Work Time: The transition to flexible working hours will also further increase due to hyper connectivity and worker demands for work-life balance. The business world is becoming increasingly stressful and two extremes are forming: "Exhaustion or "burn-out" threatens at the negative end of the spectrum. At the positive end of the spectrum is the concept of "work-life balance" (41). It is well documented however that such flexible working time contributes to the health and satisfaction of employees. Working time options such as parental leave, part-time and other leave-related arrangements are legally available to many employees, yet primarily utilized by highly-qualified employees, creating further gaps or perceptions of unfairness that need fixing.

Work Place: Due to more flexible working times, the focus also moves to a location-flexible structure of the workplace. In addition, working places are organized and created in a new way to allow for mobile work. In this context, new forms of mobile flexible collaborations are emerging, such as new office solutions, multi-space offices and home office concepts. In 2016, only one in eight employees worked from home, yet the predominant reason for this low number was the employer not offering the opportunity for home-work despite this leading to increased employee dissatisfaction. However, working from home is also associated with risks that both companies and employees should be clear about, though other studies show that employees that currently work from a home office, work comparatively more hours and are often not compensated for their overtime (42).

Work Environment: Overall, the work atmosphere is becoming increasingly characterized by a feeling of cooperation and interconnectedness. An important reason for this is the Internet, which serves as a connecting global work environment. The digital business world is thus characterized by all forms of interconnectedness, on a technical and a human level. On a technical level, this could be through the help of smarter software solutions that simplify everyday work and on a human level, this could be collaborating with colleagues in home offices or in another functional department or geographical location.

Does the Digital Age Necessitate a New Approach by Management?

With all the obvious changes brought about by digitalization and globalization, the next question for businesses is whether management itself needs to change. The changes in the business world already described exert a measurable pressure on managers to also change. The distance between managers and employees is increasing due to the increasing use of information and communication technologies, meaning managers have less opportunities to directly influence their employees. Systems need implementing to facilitate work processes and measure performance, as well as ensure effective communication. However, because of distance, the trusting relationship between managers and employees takes on an even greater importance (43), yet virtual teamwork makes it more difficult to develop trust. This simply means that for the management of the future, more focus must be on developing trust and creating trust-based teamwork. A culture of trust that requires the empowerment and self-responsibility of employees is therefore the basis for the successful implementation of the new work forms of the future (44). In a virtual context, work that is separated by time and location also requires an increased level of self-direction on the part of the team.

Trust has always been an important prerequisite for successful management. The management expert Peter Drucker commented, "organizations are no longer built on force but on trust" (10). Furthermore, Fredmund Malik listed trust as one of the six principles of effective management (11). For two decades, the concept of **transformational leadership** (45) has also highlighted that we live in a business world that is characterized by rapid change, insecurity and different challenges in which managers must create a trust-filled environment that their employees embrace.

Organizations require both more flexible organizational structures as well as managers that are in the position to inspire their employees in such a way that they can lead them through their enthusiasm as a team to reach organizational goals (46). If this is already known, why push further? This all comes back to the underlying constant of constant change. In business, it means companies always need to look beyond todays activities and innovate for an unknown future.

What to Innovate for Business Success in the Future?

Figure 14: Levels of Business Innovation

Operations, processes, products, even strategies can be copied. So, for most business, uniqueness comes from human capital and this can only be leveraged and harnessed through leadership. This reinforces the idea that if digitalization is a given "must" for all companies and across all functions, future success will come from leadership. Leadership innovation can deliver a highly engaging working environment and continue to provide sustainable competitive advantage (47). Leaders who can influence change and achieve agility, new direction and results through people, can unlock the power of human capital, even in challenging times.

Research has confirmed that leadership behaviour influences group and organizational outcomes (48). If employees are engaged, people feel better and share positive values such as decisiveness, integrity & honesty (8, 49). There is improved morale and willingness to ride out change. Good leadership also increases trust and people feel more secure in the jobs. Better communication means more openness and willingness to speak up. Company commitment comes from understanding the company objectives, purpose and seeing how to contribute. Finally, positive effects on more teamwork and less politics also result from people feeling better about what they do and where they work.

Organizational Benefits of Leadership

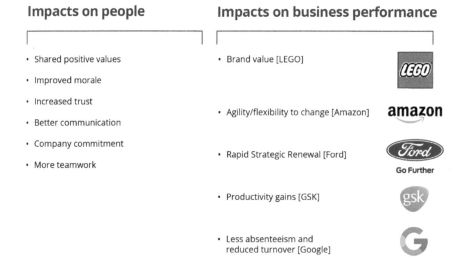

Figure 15: Examples of Organizational Benefits of Good Leadership

The bigger results can be seen from evidence that companies do better when leadership is a priority. This means going beyond the application of technology or development of innovative digital strategies and transforming organizations to achieve growth and better brand value, agility, renewal, productivity and employee engagement.

- In 2018, Lego Group brand was valued at >$7.5 billion, making it the world's most valuable toy brand. Brand value measurement is made up of factors including business performance and success credited to new CEO Niels Christiansen and his belief in digitization and authentic leadership.
- The £178 billion success, Amazon, is a good example of an agile organization able to change quickly. Leadership principles include innovation, reinvention and looking for ideas from everywhere.
- Alan Mulally is credited with saving the Ford Motor Company by leading the renewal of its strategic focus and changing Ford's risk-averse and reality-denying culture

- In 2017, Emma Walmsley was appointed new CEO of GSK. Since then, focus on productivity and termination of underperforming projects has led to Walmsley being awarded Britain's Most Admired Leader 2018 (Management Today)
- Finally, leadership and people focus are considered key success factors for Google and results are directly seen in HR statistics and employee commitment to the company.

In her book, Barbara Liebermeister (50), propagates that not everything needs to change in the digital age *"Digital doesn't matter – people remain people, management is decisive".* People remain people yet with any rapid change and uncertainty, leadership is required now more than ever. Employees are looking for stability and orientation and a more emotional side of management with the focus on ability for creating meaning, will gain importance. It is the "classical" aspects of top down management that will fall to the wayside (44). In this context, the question then becomes which competencies management in the digital age needs to concretely possess or acquire; what does leadership look like to achieve high performing organizations, teams and individuals?

Competencies of Digital Leadership

There has been much comprehensive research considering the question about what competencies or abilities are required for the digital age (51,52). The consensus includes the following:

- A "digital mindset"
- Ability to communicate
- People focus
- Ability to connect
- Creating trust
- Transparency & sharing information

Upon closer inspection of these competencies suggested for the digital age, it becomes clear that focus lies in the interaction and communication between managers and employees, hence our conviction in connectedness and the affinity between people being key. However, as personal interactions and the development of trusting relationships have always been part of true leadership, this is the point at which the concept of **Transformational Leadership** comes to the fore.

Transformational leadership, first described by Burns in 1978 (45), is well documented over many years, and has been shown to lead to higher employee satisfaction, motivation and performance (13, 53). This proven model for highly effective leadership in complex environments centres on creating a trusting basis for teamwork. With expansion to include the concept of connectedness (29), we believe it is a framework combining essential elements for the 21st century; balance of task and people orientation, courage for authenticity, kindness to others, intellectual curiosity for growth and innovation, and purpose. It is also a model and approach that can be learnt!

Key Learning Points

- Change is the only constant and as the world continues to change, businesses and leaders must change to meet these challenges and make the most of new opportunities in new working ways, global reach and technological advances
- A new approach to leadership is the key and can benefit organizational results, employee engagement and leader fulfilment
- An extended transformational leadership model, encompassing connectedness in the digital age, provides a trust-based framework for success and is one that can be learnt

Personal Reflection Points

Question 1:   What changes are you experiencing in your organization?

Question 2:   Are these similar to other organizations in your industry?

Question 3:   Reflecting on the outside world, may you expect more change in your own organization?

Question 4:   What sources of innovation could you apply in your daily work for greater competitive advantage?

Chapter 3

The Good News Is Leadership Can Be Learnt

Key Knowledge...

- Leadership is a combination of who you are, the knowledge and competencies you develop and how you behave towards others. Key elements can be learnt

- Competencies are transferable abilities which enable success in complex and unknown situations. They can be developed and strengthened and have been shown to contribute more than intelligence in determining success

- Continuous learning is not only essential for a leader's journey, it is a personal responsibility as is curiosity and a growth mind set, and required for change

Key Actions...

- Define personal goals for development of management and leadership competencies

- Take ownership of life-long learning

- Ensure all personal and team development plans follow the 70/20/10 concept with focus on new tasks, new projects and new scope for experience-based learning

Impacts...

- All managers can learn to be better leaders should they chose to take ownership for learning

- Identification of top talents through assessment of competencies for solid talent pipelines

- Effective executive development programs focused on management and leadership competencies, to prepare potential talents for future leadership roles

Much research has been undertaken in an attempt to systematically define great leadership. Is it innate, are people born a leader or is leadership effectiveness something that can be learnt? In the 1840s, Thomas Carlyle shared his Great Man Theory focused on the assumption that leaders are born, not made, and great leaders will arise when there is a great need (54). He referenced history and the impact of individuals such as Napoleon, Luther, and Shakespeare as examples of influential individuals with personal charisma, intelligence, wisdom, or political skill who used their power in a way that had a decisive impact. The counter argument at the time by Herbert Spencer however was that "such great men are the products of their societies". Either way, both arguments failed to note the gender bias and exclusion of women! The question that continued over time though was focused on the individual attributes of great leaders – what characteristics did they have, and what differentiated them from others? Even Looking more recently at Steve Jobs for example, there was much written about his leadership, yet most referred to his personality. Walter Isaacson, biographer of Jobs (55), wrote: "The essence of Jobs, I think, is that his personality was integral to his way of doing business. He acted as if the normal rules didn't apply to him, and the passion, intensity, and extreme emotionalism he brought to everyday life were things he also poured into the products he made." This focus on personality is known as "trait theories" of leadership. It may suggest what differentiates one person from another, yet can it suggest what leaders have in common? Looking beyond the simple traits or common characteristics that are often used to describe leaders, what is clear today is that leadership success comes from a combination of factors: Personality does play a part – it's who you are, a combination of values, motives, cognitions, emotional patterns and behaviours that have evolved from biological and environmental factors. Knowledge, skills and competencies to manage and lead are also essential and are acquired over time. Finally, what leaders actually do, so how you behave towards others in any given environment also counts, and this includes the ability to adapt and be situationally appropriate. This is why it is good news! Leadership can be learnt.

'Leadership and learning are indispensable to each other'

JOHN F. KENNEDY SPEECH,
PREPARED FOR DELIVERY IN DALLAS, NOVEMBER 22, 1963

The Elements for Leadership Ability

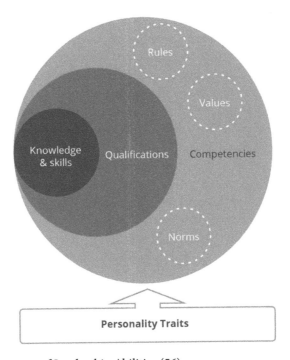

Figure 16: Elements of Leadership Abilities (56)

Our **personality**, a combination of multiple elements, drives us. Our values are principles of behaviour or judgement of what is important in life, and motives are what make us tick. These define the activities we like to do and how we like do them, through translation to feelings, thinking and behaviours. This also includes our attitudes towards self and others, our openness to experiences and our tendency towards positivity and optimism. Interesting, though motives can change through life, attitude or mind set is more difficult to alter.

Knowledge, skills and qualifications can be gained. For any job, you need skills and knowledge to give you the ability to perform a given role. For any aspiring manager and leader, we are firm advocates to "degree up". Having business qualifications is highly recommended and developing new skills through professional training improves readiness for a leadership role, as well as strengthening a CV. Key is applying newly acquired knowledge and skills in daily work. This includes taking on new or difficult assignments, building solid experience in multiple functions and global roles. The goal for such personal development however should also be a broader and more expansive horizon. This is where competencies come in.

Competencies

Competencies are transferable abilities which enable success in complex and unknown situations (57). Competencies can be developed and strengthened and are important to understand as they have been shown to contribute more than intelligence in determining success. They indicate who is more likely to do a job better, even when skills and knowledge levels may be the same. Competencies can be selected, assessed and developed. Many companies define competency frameworks as the success behaviours all their employees are expected to demonstrate. Core employee competencies, relevant for everyone, can include taking initiative, flexibility, customer orientation and team work. The competencies for management and leadership can also be defined separately. As transferable, competencies are applicable for any manager / leader, independent of functional area, with managerial and budget responsibilities. This could also include experts in higher level positions or project leaders who manage bigger projects yet do not have direct reports. Additional competencies can be added for those with a team of direct reports.

	Management	Leadership
Competencies	• Accountability • Planning & problem solving • Decision making • Strategic thinking & acting • Change management **Plus for people managers:** *Performance management* *Employee development*	• Idealized influence • Inspirational motivation • Individualized consideration • Intellectual stimulation • Integrative support
Meta-competencies	• Effective communication • Continuous learning	

Figure 17: Examples of Management and Leadership Competencies

As discussed in chapter 1, global companies need management. This therefore implies that the management competencies listed above are required by all managers. The definitions and behavioural anchors for each of these management competencies is described in chapter 13. What is important though is knowing that this list also comprises the competencies that can predict an employee's future potential and those required for shaping businesses. As such, they are key for identification of talents for employee pipeline management. The leadership competencies shown are critical for considering ability, or potential ability, to gain buy-in and trust, as would be required for those on a leadership career path.

The leadership competencies included are the elements of the expanded transformational leadership model. As with expansion to include the concept of connectedness, we believe it is a framework for leading in the digital age and all 5 elements, the 5 Is, are explored in full detail in parts 2 and 3, including what they are all about and how to apply them in your daily work. All possible as these differentiating leadership competencies can be learnt should you chose to!

As a final point, there are two meta-competencies also listed above. These are overarching competencies that are relevant to a wide range of work settings and which facilitate adaptation and flexibility on the part of people and organizations. Communication is the topic of chapter 6 and continuous learning explored here.

Continuous Learning

Continuous learning is a meta-competency for all workers. It is also associated with higher potential for success in new roles and a criterion for top talents. The cognitive dimension of leadership is also well understood. For example, Emma Walmsley, the first female CEO of a major pharmaceutical company noted her high IQ as a factor in her success as a world class leader (58). Interesting she also describes her leadership style as simple as she focuses on purpose, performance and people!

Continuous learning as a competency describes seeking ways to enhance knowledge and skills and active involvement in learning activities for personal development. It includes facing criticism and learning from mistakes, understanding and dealing with own strengths and development areas, and asking for and using feedback to improve performance. **Curiosity** is also an underlying attribute in learning, meaning being inquisitive, wondering, ready to poke around and figure something out. This requires ability and willingness to grow and change.

Stanford professor Carol Dweck calls the openness to grow and change a **growth mind set** (59). It means people seeing their abilities as learnt traits which can be developed. Such people are open to challenges and new experiences and see failure as a chance to learn. Such a growth mind set is a prerequisite in a coaching scenario. The opposite, people with a fixed mind set, see intelligence and personality as static features. For them, success is about proving talent or smartness and failure means that you just don't have what it takes. Such people tend to avoid new situations and take constructive feedback personally. People with a fixed mind set are much less receptive to coaching than those with a growth mind set.

Adult Learning Process

In terms of adult learning, it must be noted that the responsibility for learning lies with the individual! As adults, the way learning occurs is a process, but one completely reliant on the learner.

Figure 18: The Adult Learning Process'

Step one is an experience, such as an event on the job, reading a paper or attending a training. All of these examples may provide new ideas, inputs, knowledge. They do not mean anything new happens though.

Step 2 is self-reflection – this means actively taking time to consider what the skill or knowledge gap was, what went well or could have been better. Reflection can be aided by feedback, however in general it is only an individual who can choose to invest energy here.

Step 3 is the eureka moment, the actual learning – determining what needs to be done differently – what to change or how to grow.

Step 4 is also active – to apply the learning, try out a new skill or a new behaviour, have the courage to change.

It can be seen that only an individual can achieve the full learning process. Organizational opportunities can provide experiences and feedback can stimulate self-reflection yet this, and subsequent phases, can only come from the individual. The good news for learning is that when combined with a growth mind set, development becomes iterative and a life long journey for fulfilment. However, how can learning and development be structured best for individuals within an organization?

'Learning is not attained by chance;
it must be sought for with ardour and
attended to with diligence'

ABIGAIL ADAMS (60)

The 70/20/10 Learning Concept

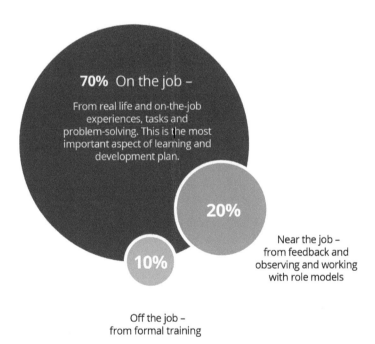

Figure 19: Representation of the 70/20/10 Learning Concept (61)

The Centre for Creative Leadership (www.ccl.org) use this formula based upon how individuals internalize and apply what they learn and how they acquire knowledge (61). The 70/20/10 learning concept highlights the contribution to our learning from **on the job experiences**. 70% of any development plan that we create for ourselves or others should include significant elements leveraging new tasks, new projects, new experiences etc. to expand competencies. This model also suggests that signing up for a training program is not the answer! Of course, trainings are beneficial to prepare employees for a new job, or to accompany them when doing so, yet focus should be on learning on the job. Only 10% is gained formally by attending training, yet to be effective, it should be combined with on the job or near job actions –otherwise newly acquired skills will soon disappear again, drowned in day-to-day work. The final 20% of development planning and learning happens near the job through interactions such as from feedback and from observing others and working with role models.

It must always be remembered however that although the task of performance management and employee development lies with the line manager, it is the individual's responsibility to keep learning. This ownership of learning is even more important in light of life-long learning associated with brain fitness and mental well-being (62). When considered alongside further changes in the work place, continuous learning is even more critical. To quote Peter Fisk, business leader and author on innovation and growth, "most people will have at least 6 different careers, requiring fundamental re-educating, whilst the relentless speed of innovation will constantly demand new skills and knowledge to keep pace, let alone give an edge." (63).

Key Learning Points

- Leadership can be learnt: knowledge and skills can be acquired, and competencies developed. The extended transformational leadership model defines the key leadership competencies for the digital age

- Continuous learning is the responsibility of the individual, is an active process requiring practice and application

- All development plans should follow the 70/20/10 learning concept

Personal Reflection Points

Question 1: From reviewing the management and leadership competencies, what are your strengths?

Question 2: Where do you see that you have development areas? What actions can you take to improve these?

Question 3: Do you have a personal development plan?

Question 4: What is your current position & career or personal goals for the next 3-5 years?

Question 5: Which of your strengths do you want to leverage and why?

Question 6: Which of your development areas or gaps versus goals / ideal future role must you work on? How will you do this and who can support you?

How to Achieve Connectedness with Self

Welcome to Part Two, the focus of which is leveraging strong self-identity as the foundation for courage to bring our true selves to the workplace.

Chapter 4

The Beauty of Transformational Leadership

Key Knowledge...

- Transformational leadership is a proven model delivering higher employee satisfaction, motivation and performance
- The 5 Is of extended transformational leadership can be considered a blue print for how to lead effectively in today's complex business world
- Based on trust, the 5 Is allow leaders to create an environment of purpose, individuality, innovation, connectedness and success

Key Actions...

- Demonstrate all elements daily to establish values and purpose in an organization
- Balance high people orientation with task focus (management competencies) to ensure achievement of the right things for the business
- Share the 5 Is principles to shape a more positive future

Impacts...

- Organizational performance
- Team trust, engagement, commitment and spirit
- Personal meaning

Transformational leadership, first described by Burns in 1978 (45), is well documented over many years, and has been shown to lead to higher employee satisfaction, motivation and performance (13). However, with massive social change, workplace changes, more remote and virtual teams and digitalization, the demand on leaders has also changed. We have examined such impacts and considered the competency profile of a leader in today's global and digital world. One key continuing theme is building a trusting environment, central to transformational leadership, yet the connectedness required today is not considered in the original model.

Based on our academic and professional experience, we have highlighted gaps and expanded the transformational leadership model from 4 to 5 Is. Our addition of "Integrative support" and new behavioural anchors updates the ideal profile of a global leader in the digital age.

The Original Concept of "Transformational Leadership"

Until today this is the most popular and scientifically researched leadership model (64, 65, 66) and therefore is viewed as the "style" of modern times. The key question that the concept of transformational leadership answers is: In a business world that is characterized by complexity and uncertainty, how can managers transfer inspiring goals and gain the trust of their employees to lead them to performance that reaches beyond the limits of their own imagination? To this end, transformational leaders set challenging goals, empower their team members and respond to individual needs and opportunities for personal development (67).

Transformational Leadership Creates Trust

Fundamentally, employees who are led by transformational leaders develop not only loyalty and respect, but also increased trust in their manager (68). This trust is developed because leaders treat their employees with integrity, commitment and fairness and place trust in them. This is demonstrated by managers giving employees increasing responsibilities and giving them more latitude for making decisions (67). In addition, numerous studies show how transformational leadership strengthens the trust of the employees amongst one another in an organizational context and thereby supports identification within a team. This creates a cooperative climate that promotes the communication and collaboration of the team members (69, 70, 71).

With increased work in virtual teams, personal contact is declining, and this presents a particular challenge for trusting relationships between managers and employees, but again research has established that transformational leaders can gain more trust, which has a positive impact on satisfaction with the leadership and group cohesion across virtual teams (68, 72).

The Original 4 Is of Transformational Leadership

Competency	Idealized Influence	Inspirational Motivation	Individualized Consideration	Intellectual Stimulation
Theme	Role modelling	Setting direction	People orientation	Challenging the status quo
Behavioural anchors	• Leading by influence • Acting authentically • Creating context • Ethical behaviour	• Building a vision • Using purpose & achievement as motivators • Speaking to inspire	• Choosing to care • Coaching others • Recognizing individual strengths & developing accordingly	• Establishing flexibility & agility in teams • Creating an environment for innovation • Leveraging diversity

Figure 20: The Traditional 4 Is of Transformational Leadership

The original model of transformational leadership comprises four elements as seen in the table. (73). These describe what a leader needs to demonstrate and how to go about it.

Idealized influence. Idealized influence is characterized by a manager's function as role model and leading by positive influence. People experience such managers as dedicated, determined and recognize outstanding characteristics. The leaders thereby gain admiration, recognition and respect.

Inspirational motivation. Inspirational motivation means that the manager successfully develops an attractive picture of the future that is transmitted through a convincing vision, communicated with confidence, ease and enthusiasm. Managers can thereby inspire their co-workers and increase their motivation and level of commitment to their work on shared objectives. This ultimately brings others on the journey and leads to a higher overall level of performance.

Individualized consideration. Individualized consideration is treating all people as individuals. Leaders are able to recognize the individual strengths, weaknesses and needs of their employees. Employees are valued as individuals and supported. Through feedback, mentoring and coaching, managers specifically support the development of individual skills and strengths. They highlight to employees their career perspectives, increase their area of responsibility and develop their potential beyond their initial role description. As a result, employees take increasing responsibility for their own development as well as for the development of the organization.

Intellectual stimulation. Intellectual stimulation develops when managers promote the questioning of established beliefs and ideas. Problems are viewed from a new perspective and viewed as a challenge in order to find new and unconventional solutions. Creative strategies and innovative problem-solving capabilities are demonstrated by the employees and potential issues, such as failure, that can accompany new and innovative approaches are tolerated alongside solutions that may deviate from the original ideas of the manager. The idea is to create an environment in which employees have the confidence to question the status quo and contribute new ideas.

Transformational Leadership in the Digital Age Including a 5th I

When viewing the concept of transformational leadership based on the aspects of management in the digital age (digital mind set, ability to communicate, people focus, ability to connect, trust and transparency), many parallels can be made. The focus on the individual and building a trusting mutual relationship is the central and pivotal point and goal of transformational leadership. Communication and transparency play a role in every aspect of transformational leadership. For example, idealized influence involves presenting oneself authentically in order to get the buy-in of employees. Inspirational motivation involves communicating goals, an attractive vision and emotionally inspiring employees to provide business context. Communication through dialogue with employees ultimately provides the basis for individualized consideration and honest feedback on performance and potential also reinforces candidness and trust. To stimulate employees intellectually, it is important to exhibit communicative conduct that provides for the active and uninhibited flow of communication, as well as sincerity to discuss negative or problematic topics and not keep them secret. It also means managers should not be the ones to always speak first and allow others to contribute.

The more "digital" relevant competencies that are not directly addressed in the concept of transformational leadership are the mind set for technology and the connectedness or networking ability, as network-based work has gained increasing importance throughout the course of digitalization. This knowledge led to our expansion of the transformational leadership model with a 5th I – Integrative Support (29).

Competencies of Extended Transformational Leadership (5 Is) in the Digital Age: A model to create an environment of trust, based around connecting with self and others.

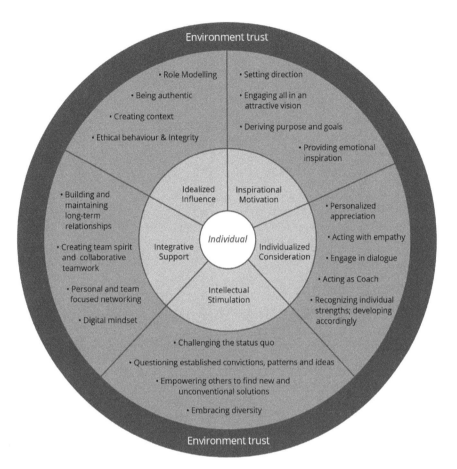

Figure 21: The Competencies of the Extended Transformational Leadership Model

In the digital and global world, leaders can extend their abilities in the following ways:

1. Building and maintaining long term relations, despite distance or virtual environments
2. Creating team spirit and collaborative teamwork across fragmented groups
3. Personal and team-focused networking
4. Leveraging a digital mind set

This 5th I, "**Integrative Support**" makes it easier to work in the digital networking economy. Managers make it easier for their employees to communicate by providing a digital mindset for the necessary infrastructure and the technical know-how. More importantly, they encourage cross-border networking and act as a role model for well-connectedness. In this way, managers support collaborative project work and create an atmosphere of openness and a "we" feeling.

Key Learning Points

- The goal of extended transformational leadership, a highly active and effective people-oriented model, is creating an environment of trust, not control
- The 5 Is of transformational leadership define the competencies and abilities managers need to successfully deliver results through people in business today
- The 5 Is consider self (idealized influence) and how to connect with others (inspirational motivation, individualized consideration, intellectual stimulation and integrative support)

Personal Reflection Points

Question 1: Have you experienced transformational leadership?

If so, how did it make you feel?

Is it an environment in which you believe that you would flourish in and why?

Question 2: Do you consider transformational leadership a style you use or could use more? How could you go about this?

Chapter 5

It Starts From Individuals

Key Knowledge...

- Whenever we consider leadership, it is clear that it starts from the individual, choosing to step forward, choosing to set aside ego for others and choosing to do so with generosity and kindness
- Self-awareness, self-reflection and self-development are fundamental for the leadership journey
- Personal values and motives drive how we feel, think and behave (communicate). This impacts others, good or bad, and the moment we lose emotional control and behave inappropriately, we lose the ability to steer decisions, influence and lead people.

Key Actions...

- Develop skills and competencies associated with emotional intelligence and effective communication
- Engage others in decision making, augment own thinking, share ideas and leverage more collaborative problem solving
- Demonstrate positive behaviours associated with effective communication, including understanding styles, adaptability, situational sensitivity and choosing to engage others in dialogue

Impacts...

- Self-awareness helps leaders discover and live the impact they want to have, on their teams and organizations
- People with high emotional intelligence are usually successful in most things they do, they show complete trust in others, they care for others, make others feel good by building rapport, and they are better at dealing with stress
- Effective communication, the foundation for successful leadership, reduces conflict resulting from misunderstandings and increases engagement and motivation of teams.

Not only can leadership be learnt, transformational leadership can be applied by anyone to positively influence others in teams or in projects, by beginning to change the way *you* behave. This is because leadership starts from the individual.

Figure 22: The Expanding Scope of Leadership

Throughout a career or within an organization, leaders' responsibility and scope may expand from simply working in a team to managing and developing teams. The focus and tasks may differ, yet the foundation is still the individual leader, beginning with intrapersonal understanding and self- development.

Personal Drivers

We are all highly complex individuals, yet for leaders, who they are, what they do and how they do it is looked at, judged and often criticized by those around them, both above and below. Leaders are also looked upon for guidance, direction and support. It is essential that anyone desiring influence or a leadership position must know themselves, how they come across and how they interact and build relationships with others. **Self-awareness** is true knowledge of one's own character and feelings, and understanding our emotions and behaviours in decision making, relationship building, driving productivity and delivering on goals and results. Sadly, surveys have shown many people do not show high self-awareness (74) and self-reflection, yet many teachings related to emotional intelligence and emotional stability indicate this insight is fundamental for personal change and growth (62, 75, 76, 77, 78). Self-awareness is a key starting point for having a conscious knowledge of ourselves, including the ability to form an accurate self-concept and the impact we have on others. Self-reflection is fundamental in learning, such as considering one's own role in situations, showing willingness to seek feedback and to grow more. Self-reflection or observation makes self-responsibility possible. Only when we take responsibility for personal performance can we truly develop self-control. Such a level of self-control includes holding back unhelpful impulses and remaining positive and unflustered even under stressful conditions. It also requires authenticity, flexibility and accountability to objectives, promises and clearing up miscommunications when necessary.

'Know thyself'

INSCRIPTION ON THE TEMPLE OF APOLLO AT DELPHI

Looking in-depth starts with understanding personal drivers and the connections between them. We need to start deep in the often-hidden areas to see how what we express to others is driven by how we feel and think. **Values** are our principles of behaviour or judgement of what is important in life, and motives are what make us tick. For example, intrinsic motivations guide our career choices and define the

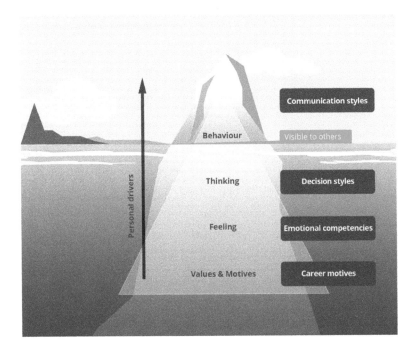

Figure 23: **Personal Drivers**

activities we like to do and how we do it (78). Motives and feelings are key drivers that shape how we think, make decisions and solve problems. Strong emotional competencies are required by leaders for managing own and others' feelings and in turn impact behaviours; what we say and what we do. Through the translation from values to feelings, thinking and behaviours we impact others.

Career Motives

Being aware of what makes us tick can help guide the choices we make in careers and find the best fit for the types of roles or organizations we consider. Low fit leads to dissatisfaction and poor performance! Four career paths have been mapped to career motives (79); expert, linear, spiral & transitory.

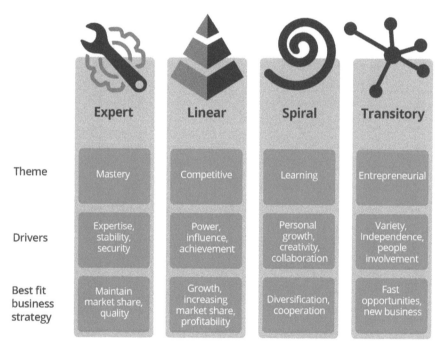

	Expert	Linear	Spiral	Transitory
Theme	Mastery	Competitive	Learning	Entrepreneurial
Drivers	Expertise, stability, security	Power, influence, achievement	Personal growth, creativity, collaboration	Variety, Independence, people involvement
Best fit business strategy	Maintain market share, quality	Growth, increasing market share, profitability	Diversification, cooperation	Fast opportunities, new business

Figure 24: Representation of Four Career Paths Behind Career Motives

"Expert" can be likened to a traditional craft career path based on mastery of one craft. Drivers include stability and security and best fit is to a role or company focused on steadiness, often with flat structures and performance measures related to accuracy and technical expertise.

The "linear" path is based on a military career with progression up the ladder or to the top of the pyramid, to attain more power or influence. Performance is driven by achievement and promotion. Such motives work well in businesses focused on growth and increasing market share.

"Spiral" paths reflect changes in the workplace over the last 20-30 years. It is no longer the case that work is all about workers and managers. Those with spiral motives have a focus on life-long learning, both for themselves and others hence their careers show moves laterally and vertically for development rather than power. They do well in expanding environments, especially where collaboration is required for innovation.

The "transitory" motives and career path is also a more modern development, more associated with project management type roles; short term, full of variety and fast moving.

Not only do career motives guide where we put our energies, they also indicate what we care about and where we are more likely to thrive. For example, an expert is unlikely to thrive in a broader role such as a general manager which requires a high linear and spiral profile, though head of a speciality area may show high expert and linear motives. The challenge is strong self-awareness on our personal motive, and not just what we believe we should be (our conditioned beliefs), but what our heart really tells us we want!

Emotional Competencies

Discussing feelings may not be a natural focus when we consider management and leadership, yet research has shown that great leaders demonstrate strong emotional competencies and high emotional intelligence (75, 76). Emotional intelligence, a learnt ability to engage, motivate and influence others, is important because people with high emotional intelligence are usually successful in most things they do. This reflects how they deal with own and others' feelings; in other words, how successfully leaders manage their own emotions, anticipate reactions, and understand the best interpersonal style to adopt to be most effective in social or emotional situations.

For many of the emotional competencies proven to be crucial for effective leadership, interestingly women have been proven to have better levels than men. Research by the Hays Group found that "women outperform men in 11 of 12 key emotional intelligence competencies crucial for effective leadership" (80). This data came from 55,000 professionals across 90 countries and also supports the general concept of emotional competencies required by leaders. They found that women demonstrated better self-awareness, empathy, coaching and mentoring, influence, inspiration, conflict management, organizational awareness, adaptability, team-work and achievement orientation. Women only scored slightly higher than men in positive outlook and emotional self-control was the only competency in which men and women showed equal performance.

> 'Emotional Intelligence is twice as important
> for excellent performance as technical skills
> and conventional IQ'
>
> DANIEL GOLEMAN (75)

Having high emotional intelligence ensures the right actions – it is choosing actions for beneficial outcomes, and this can be learnt. It is about learning to manage our own emotions and those of others because our actions and decisions are based on emotion (how we feel) and cognition (what we think) and, therefore impact others. The challenge however is the power of unchecked emotions, especially under stress because the moment you lose emotional control, you lose the ability to steer decisions, influence and lead people. Whenever we are feeling sad, bad or mad, we are unable to make good decisions. When tired, people often do or say the wrong things. It is because they are not thinking straight. Its why some people handle conflict and stress better than others.

The science bit – emotions can have a physiological effect before we understand what we feel and can therefore hijack rational thinking and result in poor actions (75). The amygdala and prefrontal cortex of the brain both support processes that are important for the expression and regulation of the emotional response to stress (246). Though there is individual variability in stress responses, for many, in high emotional states the complex prefrontal cortex shuts down and the amygdala takes over for rapid reactions. This fight, flight or freeze survival instinct is still very powerful and if left unchecked can lead to poor reactions. On the other hand, those with high emotional intelligence are able to overcome this quick impulsive response and employ rational thought, such as in low emotional states, when the prefrontal cortex can perceive, control and evaluate emotions and to use this information to guide thinking and actions. This is known as emotional separation, enabling inner calm in difficult circumstances and retention of the ability to think rationally and take high quality decisions.

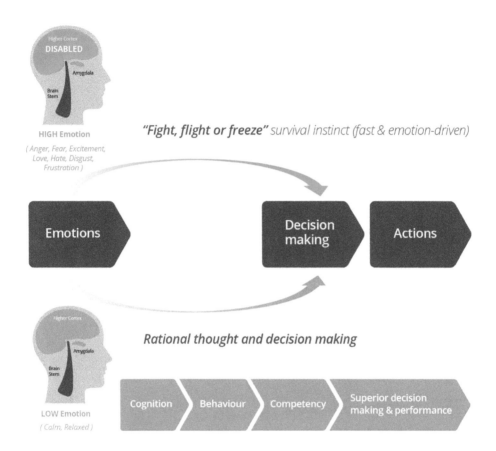

Figure 25: Representation of Brain Functions in Emotional Intelligence

In summary, **emotional intelligence** refers to the ability to perceive, control and evaluate emotions and Goleman, the "father" of emotional intelligence, defined 5 elements to frame this ability towards self and other people and to measure it (75):

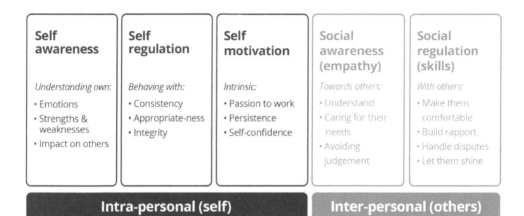

Figure 26: The Elements of Emotional Intelligence

The intrapersonal elements are what goes on inside you, and the interpersonal, what goes on between you and other people. These two sides relate to balancing personal reactions and the mood or emotional subtleties of others. Assessment of many experts and individual contributors in the work place often show high intra-personal ability. Leaders however need to score well on all five elements, especially the inter-personal as these are critical for engaging others successfully and building rapport. Commercial tools are available to measure Emotional Quotient (EQ) and we highly recommend leaders utilize these for self-reflection and development.

In summary, strong "self" or intrapersonal intelligence is linked to sureness in one's self:

	Key aspects	Opportunity	Visible signs	Development areas	Outcomes
"Self" elements • Awareness • Regulation • Motivation	Understanding own actions, emotions & underlying reasons	Thinking before acting	• Calm under pressure • Look at problems objectively & find solutions • Take criticism well • Optimism & confidence	Cognitive skills: • Slowing down to avoid impulsive behaviour & challenging reactions • Self-reflection	Careful, informed decisions: the right actions, even under stress

Figure 27: Summary of "Self" Elements of Emotional Intelligence

Development of the "others" elements of interpersonal intelligence, also known as social intelligence is paramount for connecting with others and building rapport, and from a leadership perspective for sharing a sense of importance. It can also go so far as to bring care and compassion in to the workplace by making others feel important. Through understanding other people and their behaviour, assumptions, judgements and stereotyping can be avoided and through treating people as valued individuals, people are engaged, motivated and more committed at work. It's a win-win!

	Key aspects	Opportunity	Visible signs	Development areas	Outcomes
"Others" elements • Empathy • Social skills	Understanding other people & their behaviour	Engaging people	• Openness to others /ideas • Speaking kindly, listening • Building rapport • Showing compassion	Communication skills: • Body language • Responding to feelings • Sharing praise • Dealing with conflicts	Better relations, trust and lasting influence

Figure 28: **Summary of "Others" Elements of Emotional Intelligence**

Decision Styles

Decision making is an important competency for managers and senior employees with budget or project responsibility and as such must be understood and developed. It is a key example of our thinking approach, alongside how we solve problems and how we plan. Using decision making as an example, it helps us also understand that it is linked to our motives, feelings and hence behaviours. Though decision making is a cognitive process of identifying and choosing alternatives, and logically should be based on knowledge, skills and experience, it is influenced by the values, preferences and beliefs of the decision-maker. More importantly, how we make decisions should also reflect the situation and how we include those around us. In organizations, it has also been shown that successful senior managers have the ability to use different decision styles in different situations and the mix of styles they employ also change with their level of responsibility (81).

So, what do you need to know about decision making? Firstly, never accept the argument that there is not enough information.... Being the leader means there are times you have to decide one way or the other and continuing to seek out more and more information does not help and there is such a thing as information overload (82):

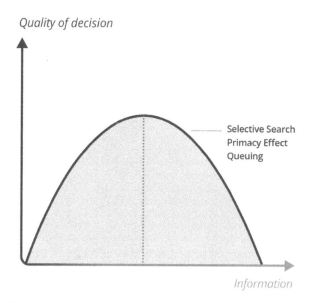

Figure 29: Illustration of Information Overload

When is information or knowledge too much versus when is there enough for effective decision making? The paradox behind this problem is the general assumption that the greater the availability of information, the better the quality of the decision will be. This is a fallacy. The quality of a decision is often impaired by the availability of too much information. Various psychological theories explain how a high degree of information can lead to poor decision quality:

Selective information search: If a large amount of information is available about a certain topic, it is necessary to focus in on a few key pieces and in most cases, individuals search for information which supports their previous assumptions, as opposed to information which refutes them.

Primacy Effect: As a rule, individuals tend to view the last piece of information they read as most important. Though it is simply more present in the brain, and subconsciously, decisions are more influenced by the recent information as opposed to information which arrived at an earlier time.

Queuing: When very high volumes of information are being processed, newly arriving information will be initially pushed to one side.

In addition to the amount of information we prefer for decision making, our style is further complicated by what is done with the information or our solution focus.

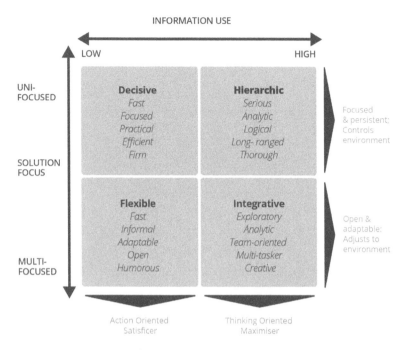

Figure 30: Representation of Decision-Making Styles from the Leadership Insights Assessment

In this application of style in the Leadership Insight Assessment® from Decision Dynamics LLC (83), another useful assessment tool commercially available, "Information Use" refers to the amount of information or knowledge we use to reach a decision. "Solution Focus" describes what is ultimately done with the information or knowledge gathered. The interesting point is that there are no right or wrong styles, however different styles are appropriate for different situations.

There are 4 styles seen here that represent an individual's behaviour and thinking pattern that influence decision making and problem solving and impact on success in business and with others.

Decisive style: Low information use and uni-focused solutions is a good approach in simple, clear environments due to a drive for actions and efficiency. Decision making is fast, based on grabbing a few key facts and deciding on one course of action. On the downside, such individuals risk going it alone, ignoring complexity and jumping to action too quickly.

Flexible style: Low information use and multi-focused solutions is effective when adaptability and agility are required. Decisions can be made with little information yet willingness to improvise and keeping options open shows resourcefulness in situations with low clarity. On the flipside, too many ideas mean planning may not be detailed enough or only have a short-term perspective.

Hierarchic style: High information use and uni-focused solutions is associated with high detail orientation and analysis of much complex data. It can appear logical, seeking to optimize ideas in complex situations, yet focus on one solution limits perspectives and new alternatives. It can result is too much control.

Integrative style: High information use and multi-focused solutions works well in high complexity and can help paint the big picture. It is linked with exploring new ideas, finding new creative possibilities and setting out many options. This however will slow actions and can appear indecisive.

Having awareness of how you make decisions can help reflect on habits and suggest opportunities for more variety both in personal style and when to include other people more. Understanding the way other people use information and knowledge to make decisions and generate solutions can help collaborations and actively seeking perspectives from those with different styles can enhance creating thinking. As mentioned, the ability to utilize different styles is also important in career progression. Analysis of leaders has shown that styles change through organizational levels, for example a supervisor often demonstrates a decisive style, possibly based on a perceived need to make quick operation decisions alone and then tell others what to do. A CEO on the other hand with focus on long term strategy, risk management and responsibility for company success requires the ability to use all 4 styles, adapting as necessary to complexity, time and people.

Communication Styles

Good and effective communication is an essential tool for achieving productivity and maintaining strong, lasting working relationships. Studies have shown that 80 to 90 percent of the average leader's week is spent communicating (84). Doing this well is therefore paramount. Effective communication is also a competency all employees need to master as it is a meta-competency (57), enabling success in complex and unknown situations and relevant in a wide range of work settings, and essential for collaborative decision making and sharing decisional outcomes. A definition of effective communication includes thinking with clarity and expressing ideas, facts, information and knowledge consistently. It is also about choosing appropriate language a multitude of differing audience types will best understand.

Despite the vital need for communication in business, as well as our personal lives, skills and abilities in this area can still be a barrier (85). Individuals need to be willing to use all modes of communication (86) to engage others: Informing, questioning, appreciating, complaining (with recommended changes) and sharing wishes, hopes and dreams. Limited use narrows the quality of dialogue. We must also never assume that how we like to communicate is the best for the receiver and interpersonal adaptability is key here. Especially when it comes to the volume of information or detail given, as well as the format, speed and focus.

> *'The single biggest problem in communication*
> *is the illusion that it has taken place'*
>
> GEORGE BERNARD SHAW (118)

Communication is also the foundation to expand and be successful in all other areas of leadership and is a key area for life long development. Most conflict results from misunderstandings and poor communication between people (87). Engagement and motivation stem from trust and open communication. In this context, this means leaders firstly understanding their own communication style, then understanding the style and needs of others and lastly being aware of the situation, all to ensure communication is as effective as possible.

Our communication style reflects how we are perceived by others. As it is an observable behaviour, the image we give may be different from how we believe we come across. Our first impressions may not be ideal! Communication can be unconscious or conscious. At times we knowingly adopt a different style when dealing with people as we actively aim to motivate and influence others or when attempting to behave as we believe we should, such as in presentations, meetings, interviews and when meeting people for the first time. Again, like with decision styles, there is no right and wrong with communication style, yet leaders should be aware of their natural style and practice being more versatile when communication with other people.

Many methodologies and tools are available to assess communication styles. Once such example is DISC (88) which looks at observable behaviours and "how" people act. It is a simple approach measuring two dimensions: how people make decisions and whether people are introverts or extroverts. Four profiles then describe the characteristics and tendencies such people demonstrate naturally.

Thinking/logical decision making:

Task Oriented
Direct Communication Style

Introvert:
Reserved &
Slow Paced

Extrovert:
Outgoing &
Fast Paced

Feeling/emotional decision making:

People Oriented
Indirect Communication Style

Figure 31: Representation of Communication Styles from DISC Methodologies

D= dominance (red): Describes someone fast, task oriented, who wants results. This type of person may appear proactive and decisive and tends to communicate in a very direct, sometimes too telling manner.

I = influence (yellow): It describes a person motivated by relationships. This person may be a strong networker, persuasive, optimistic and futuristic. Their style of communication is informal, wanting to connect to people before getting down to business. As they may like to discuss lots of ideas, they may appear unstructured to others.

S = steadiness (green): A quieter person, a strong team player and one that needs more reassurance in communications. They are also dependable, supportive, loyal, systematic and a good listener, though not always willing to speak up in noisy environments.

C = compliance or conscientiousness (blue): People motivated to act in environments of rules and procedures. As such they are detail oriented, analytical, accurate, and focused on quality. They want facts, are formal in communication yet need time to analyze to make rational choices. For others, this can be perceived as slow and hindering quick actions.

Such a tool is useful to explore personal behavioural or communication styles, to learn to recognize the communication style of others and then learn to adapt and blend styles for more effective communication and relationships. Interpersonal adaptability relates to the inclination to adapt to different people and circumstances and modify behaviour to relate to others better. It is not about being un-authentic, it is about having a toolbox of skills and versatility to act in a manner that the other person will be more receptive to. For example, going back to DISC, if a leader is naturally more of an influencer (yellow), they will need to communicate in a more direct and specific manner and deliver more facts to a blue type person to engage them.

A leader can learn to choose to be versatile, adapting their own style to enable more effective communication. Tools like this can also be used to learn how best to communicate as a team with focus on valuing the diversity of different styles, solution-oriented communication and creating a stimulating and successful working environment.

'No one is born with all the skills to deal with the challenges of life and the people we encounter, yet we can all keep learning to do better'

PAUL MCGEE (87)

Key Learning Points

- We are shaped by our values, motives, feelings and thinking and these are translated into behaviours or actions that others experience

- Leaders must show high self-awareness, self-regulation and self-development as part of life-long learning, because of the impact they have on others

- Emotional intelligence is critical for success in many situations. Individual contributors may demonstrate high intrapersonal, "self" elements, yet leaders also require high interpersonal, "others" elements, to engage people, as well as more effective decision making and handling of stressful situations

- How we make decisions and communicate are key business competencies; both can be developed and adapted for effectiveness

Personal Reflection Points

Question 1: Do you take time away from daily tasks for self-reflection?

Question 2: What makes you tick?

Question 3: What do you like about your current job? What would you change?

Question 4: What are your strengths that you leverage in your daily work? What are your development areas so you could be even better?

Question 5: Can you begin to see new ways that you can define for yourself to becoming a better leader?

Chapter 6
Achieving Personal Impact and Influence

Key Knowledge...

- Impact is to have a marked effect on someone or something
- Influence is the power to cause someone to change a behaviour, belief, or opinion, based on motivation and common vision
- Central to establishing impact and influence is personal attitude, presence and ability

Key Actions...

- Build two-trust, forged and maintained through effective communication and consistent delivery
- Utilize referent and expert power (personal power), not formal power or coercion to drive actions
- Create common ground and shared visions for others to be able to achieve buy-in
- Leverage positive personal presence

Impacts...

- Positive first and lasting impressions in the minds of others
- Positive identity and professional respect
- A managed and consistently delivered personal brand

Impact is to have a marked effect and influence is to affect a change. For a leader it is about achieving positive personal impact and long term, lasting influence in business. Influence especially is essential, beyond positions and titles, as it is about motivating people to work together toward making the vision a reality. It is not coercion. It is based on personal abilities such as effective communication, emotional intelligence, but is also strongly linked to image or personal brand. This chapter explores how impact and influence is created and translated into business results.

What are the Key Dimensions to Influence Others in Business?

In time-sensitive circumstances, persuasion techniques may be useful for expediting results, however, in most situations, influence is the preferred means to a productive end. This is because influence is based on trustful relationships that have been solidified over time.

So, what are the different elements that impact our ability to influence especially if we have no direct or formal authority? These can include how we come across, our presence, our business persona; whether we are credible, based on our skills, knowledge and expertise; if we are known for having a proven track record for performance and delivery; who we know, who we are networked with and how we form coalitions; if we are seen to respect and value differences, and actively consider the interests of others; do we have awareness for and show respect for power structure; and there may be others dependent on the situation and individuals involved (89, 90, 91). However, the core elements of influence can be narrowed to power, trust and understanding, as these frame relationships (89).

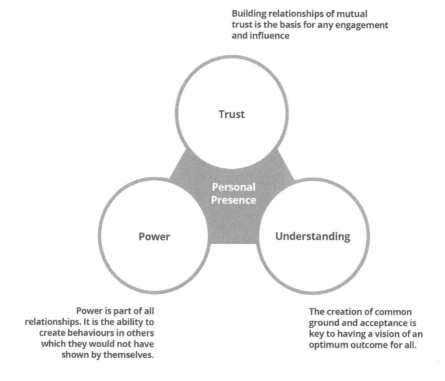

Figure 32: The Core Elements of Influence

Trust is the basis and prerequisite for engagement and influence. Power cannot be ignored as is part of all relationships and is the ability to create behaviours in others which they would not have shown by themselves. Lastly, understanding others to create common ground and acceptance is key to having a vision of an optimum outcome for all, and moving towards that shared vision, even when starting goals may be different. This would be particularly true in a negotiation situation. To translate this theoretical model into meaning, the dimensions will be considered here one by one.

Trust: The Precursor to Engagement and Influence

We have used the word trust multiple times already as it is the goal of transformational leadership to create an environment of trust. But what exactly is trust? The definition says: it is "a psychological state comprising the intention to accept vulnerability based upon positive expectations of the intentions or behaviour of another" (92). In other words, allowing **vulnerability**, to speak openly about a mistake for example, because the expectation is that the other person will react in a positive way. This means trust allows people to be honest with each other and to show their weaknesses as well as strengths, without fear of recrimination or abuse.

In a business environment, trust is a crucial precursor to gain positive engagement. The evidence from transformational leadership shows that the **environment of trust** that is created by such leaders really does result in "higher employee satisfaction, motivation and performance" (13). Furthermore, as management guru Peter Drucker put it, it's a duty as "organizations are no longer built on force but on trust. The existence of trust between people does not necessarily mean that they like each other. It means they understand one another. Taking responsibility for relationships is therefore an absolute necessity. It is a duty" (93).

In addition, trust impacts how communication is perceived because of the relationship aspect. As the renowned communication scientist Watzlawick stated, "every communication has a content and relationship aspect such that the latter classifies the former" (94). Trust works on the relationship aspect here and has an impact on how we perceive the other person. One simple example to demonstrate. Imagine a manager tells you: "I'd like to discuss your area of responsibility, maybe we can shift a few things around". If you don't trust that manager, you would probably react in a negative way, afraid you've done something wrong, suspecting that your manager is trying to punish you…On the other hand, if you trust the manager, you'll be more open to discuss options as you expect positive actions from him or her. This shows how trustful relationships strongly influence how we understand anything the other person is telling us.

The question is how can **trustful relationships** be built? Again, effective communication is key. As Zeffane and colleagues found in studies in 2011, "trust and commitment do not just happen; they are forged and maintained through effective communication" (95). For example, how employees perceive their communication with management has one of the strongest effects on a company's trust climate. Communication channels have to work well, otherwise misunderstandings and misrepresentations set in, and with them mistrust. Messages must also communicate competence and be consistent, and the sender must show integrity and benevolence (look after the interests of others) in order to build trust.

So, trust makes a big difference in the relationship between two individuals, yet more than that, it has been proven to affect overall business outcomes too. According to a review from the UK government (96), trust creates 12% greater customer loyalty, 50% fewer sick days, 87% less likely to leave the organization, 18% greater productivity and 16% greater profit margin!

Based on these more general ideas on trust, let's explore specific topics of how to build trust:

Negotiating and persuading to gain influence: In many business scenarios such as management or selling, it could be seen that the goal is to persuade someone else to your way of thinking. However, this is not the case if you want a long-term relationship with the other party. This is because persuasion can be used to spur someone to action or to make a decision without actually earning their sincere buy-in which then feels like manipulation. For lasting influence, we need to go beyond persuasion and coercion and affect a change or bring about a solution in a new way. To begin to understand these differences and how to positively influence others, it is important to understand the psychological principles, mechanisms and goals.

As said, influence is the power to have a positive effect on people, to cause someone to change a behaviour, belief, or opinion, or to cause something to be changed. To affect or change how someone or something develops, behaves, or thinks. Influence is having a vision of the optimum outcome for a situation or organization and then, without using force or coercion, motivating people to work together toward making the vision a reality.

According to Cialdini, studies on persuasion have shown six principles that guide human behaviour and can be applied to increase effectiveness in business as they impact people's desire to follow or say yes (97, 98). These are *scarcity* – a critical factor to drive decisions and actions, especially in a selling scenario; *reciprocity* – meaning an obligation to give back when we receive; *authority* – people following the lead of credible, knowledgeable experts, especially when the authority is visible (for instance, people are more likely to give cash to strangers in a uniform than to people casually dressed); *consensus* – people following the actions of other similar people, so in leadership, role modelling makes a difference; **liking** – people say yes more easily to people who are similar, have common ground and cooperate. Finally, number 6, people are more easily persuaded by *consistency* of messages.

In other words, persuasion can be described as a process aimed at changing a person's attitude or behaviour toward some event, idea, object, or other person, by using written or spoken words to convey information, feelings, or reasoning. The goal or outcome is to spur someone to action or to make a decision. This can clearly be demonstrated in selling situations. Selling is a process and includes persuading a customer to accept the merits of your product or solution on offer. Management is also a process of doing the right things. Focus too is on setting goals and controlling tasks and people. It produces order and consistency by being highly task oriented. High task orientation also emphasises directive hierarchy and transaction between manager and employees based on achieving results and can include formal power and persuasion to drive actions.

Building Coalitions has also been defined as a way of establishing trust and influence (89, 90, 91). This is based on the natural force of several people collectively advocating an idea being better able to exert influence than one person alone. To assemble a powerful coalition, it is important to consider who is impacted and who's buy-in must you obtain and actively include people.

Creating Acceptance: Business today has dramatically changed due to globalization, digitalization, plus social and economic development. Management styles have therefore evolved, and influence is increasingly relevant to meet the demands of today. Influence and impact can come from outside of hierarchy, reflecting the decline of static organizational structures. Vertical reporting lines are being replaced by matrix structures and project teams. The idea of separation and arms-length relationships with other functions, suppliers and even customers have also gone. Upward flow of information and downward flow of decisions and directives is also a thing of the past. Behaviours that are impacted include decision making and problem-solving, enabling more collaborative and creative approaches. This is critical for more flexible project work and can directly lead to faster innovation. Going beyond persuasion to creating influence is therefore seeking long term and genuine buy-in to a vision or aligned goals. For example, strategic selling has a goal of relationship building with customers, rather than a one-off sale. And leadership is about inspiring others to be engaged and committed to work and personal success. It is creating an environment in which others can succeed and going beyond managing tasks to achieving results through people. It starts from building a vision to achieve common goals. It is also not linked to the title "manager" or telling others what to do.

The second dimension of influence is power, and understanding power structures, networking and goal alignment can help in creating impact through influence.

Power: The Ability to Direct the Behaviour of Others

Power cannot be ignored as it is part of all relationships and it is associated with the ability to create behaviours in others which they would not have shown by themselves. It is important to understand personal power, as well as who holds power in the workplace. And as we considered in chapter 1, is power a bad thing? According to Niklas Luhmann, famous sociologist, "power is a medium to arrange the decision criteria of a society and to ensure decidability" (24). Power facilitates decision making and those deciding set the future direction. It is also associated with responsibility, yet it does create boundaries.

Understanding Power Structures: When we consider influence, we need to once again differentiate between formal power, such as defined in a senior role, and personal power (25). Referent and expert power are examples of **personal powers**. Referent power comes from being trusted and respected for what we do and how we handle situations. Expert power comes from our experience, skills or knowledge and how that is also utilised by others. It is these examples that highlight that leadership is possible without formal directive and linked to actions. However, knowing where power comes from is important for knowing how to use it to drive decision making and influence others, and with the increasing relevance of **informal leadership** today, it is important to consider how to leverage our own inputs and the contribution of others , as well as enhance our abilities to influence the behaviour of others based on trust and respect.

It must be noted though that leaders also require a respect for structure. All organizations have structure and formal teams, and with that responsibility and decision-making authority. Yet there are often other power structures to be cognitive of. For example, management teams have significant decision-making powers due to formal structure, yet a strong trade union or workers' council may also be able to derail or sanction decisions. Understanding the sensitivities in organizations is sometimes wise. To quote Voltaire (1694-1778), "if you want to know who has the power, just ask yourself whom you should not criticize". The reason for this is not about politics, it is about understanding that others have different interests that often need to be considered.

Networking is a key skill required for indirect influence and lateral leadership (90). Not only should leaders seek to build a team around them (formal or informal) for diversity, to balance personal weaknesses and to challenge thinking, access to business networks are also important. Networking is the establishment of mutually beneficial relationships with other people to exchange ideas and build knowledge. This exchange from within an organization or from outside can include seeking out those who can help you carry out important initiatives.

Finally, **Goal Alignment** is critical when authority to direct or reprioritize is missing. A challenge for example with project teams is over-burdening team members with new tasks. When trying to influence in such a setting, motivating people to work together toward making the vision a reality can be achieved by aligning goals and giving freedom to operate to achieve them. It must be noted however that all too often focus on business goals misses consideration of personal goals where conflicts can also arise.

The third dimension of influence is understanding the interests of others and this also circles back to creating acceptance.

Understanding the Interests of Others

Understanding others, to create common ground for a solution and acceptance of ideas and concepts, is the final key to influence and shape agreement and outcomes (89). Once understood, steps can be taken. For acceptance and buy-in, people need to firstly know why you want their support, what's in it for them and does this offer or idea meet their needs? Secondly, they need to share the vision that is being offered and agree it is mutually beneficial. Thirdly, they need relevant information to make their final decision. In other words, once again it's all about how you communicate with others.

Understanding others means taking time to consider their interests, perspectives and needs. It starts with an openness and willingness to do so – **attitude** of the leader counts (99). It also includes integrating different perspectives and **valuing diversity.** It is followed by genuine dialogue. However, in business, most dialogue is technical, relating to facts, tasks, action. Discussions can go a bit further yet tend to focus on defending views. What leaders need to engage in is **genuine dialogue** and genuine dialogue only occurs when each person really has the other in mind. They use all elements of communication, questioning and listening to understand, appreciating, recommending, informing and sharing information (86). The key skills to develop are questioning and listening. Asking thoughtful questions shows sincerity and builds trust because it actively shows an interest in someone's opinions and thoughts. Listening validates others and shows respect. From this understanding of the interests of others, their needs for the given situation can be integrated and incorporated for best outcomes. Steps can be taken to actively create acceptance for the idea, decision or action desired by *how* the solution is presented. There are then three needs of others that must be met for acceptance: communicating why they need to care, the vision they need to buy in to and the information they need to decide. A common mistake is to jump into details and talk at people. It is natural as most work communication is detailed and operational, focused on what to do, how to do, who does it by when etc.

Finally, as we are seeking long term influence in business, any project or relationship does not end when the agreement is achieved. Nurturing relationships requires **feedback loops**. This is collecting inputs, even complaints, from internal or external partners to draw attention to issues and create new solutions. Such an approach can be used to improve working environments and cultivate higher customer retention.

Although trust, power and understanding are the core elements framing relationships and influence, it can be seen that the common thread connecting them is communication. Trust must be well established over time through consist communication, delivering on promises and proving your track record. Utilizing power positively comes from not coercing and overusing authority, but from leveraging the contribution of all which again centres on the collaboration, integration of others and respect for differences. Learning to appreciate and understand the interests of the other parties and actively integrating their views into a shared vision can also only work through dialogue. When it comes down to winning hearts and minds, communication is what counts – it is two-way communication to gather what is important to others and then positioning ideas and concepts in a way that people want to listen and are inspired to act. For a leader to achieve this it also goes back to understanding communication styles and leveraging emotional intelligence as the booster for human interactions. Yet, it must be remembered that communication is just one competency. Successful people are characterized by their actions, abilities (skills and competencies), attitude (linked to values and motives) and the final element, **personal presence**.

Personal Presence: This Includes Image and Dressing for Success!

Presence is not only about being present; it is also about the whole image we portray and as the saying goes "first impressions count" and impressions individuals give to others greatly influence how they are viewed and treated at work (100). It is because, as humans, we are programmed to make quick judgements, yet the biggest influencer, appearance (101), is the easiest to change, making it inexcusable to not dress for success! For anyone wishing to build impact and reputation, ascend the corporate ladder or be taken seriously as a business partner, you must be cognitive of human brain function and biases, and consider why what you wear makes a difference. When taken as a whole, understanding how the brain works, how people judge and how people can be persuaded, those wishing to be taken seriously in the business world and make it as senior managers have to dress the part, act the part and behave consistently, in other words how people expect managers to behave. It is not conforming per se, it is visible professionalism, building respect and, most importantly, trust.

First Impressions Count as They Last

Business attire has changed significantly over recent years, yet too many people have forgotten why proper business attire is important. This may sound old fashioned, especially in today's world of t-shirt-wearing tech CEOs such as Mark Zuckerberg, yet those wishing to build impact and reputation must be cognitive of human brain function and biases linking appearance and competency.

'The eye sees only what the mind is prepared to comprehend'

ROBERTSON DAVIES (102)

The idea of a professional **business persona** relates to both self-image and projected image. Especially important for women is the perception we create of ourselves, as this has a strong influence on how we are seen. So yes, it does matter what we wear to work if we want to be taken seriously as a manager or leader. Have you ever wondered why airports are full of men in suits on a Monday morning? The colour may vary; some are dressed in black suits, some in dark blue and some in different shades of grey. This procession is usually repeated on Friday night flights as well, dedicated to commuting managers, consultants etc. If you look at senior management meetings you will find the same picture. Why? It's a uniform. To quote Grayson Perry, "when he dons a uniform, a man takes on a bit of the power of all men who wear that uniform" (103). What does this mean for women or up and coming managers? Unfortunately, if you want to be part of a crowd, you have to look and act the part. Therefore, creating your own professional business persona is a key development step.

Research has revealed 67 per cent of bosses turn down applicants as a result of their inappropriate dress sense (104). According to TheLadders.co.uk, men turning up for interviews with no tie, a t-shirt and jeans were deemed as some of the biggest fashion offences to employers, while women wearing dangly jewellery failed to make the cut. Flashing bare legs in mini-skirts also failed to help women land a career, with bosses opting in favour of candidates in mid-length hemlines.

A first impression is the event when one person first encounters another person and forms a mental image of that person (100). Impression accuracy varies depending on the observer and the target (person, object, scene, etc.) being observed. First impressions are based on a wide range of characteristics: age, race, culture, language, gender, physical appearance, accent, posture, voice, number of people present, and time allowed to process. The challenge though is two-fold: the mental image is made in only 7 seconds and we really can't trust our brains.

Believe it or not, our decisions are not always our own thanks to the **unconscious biases** buried in our brains (105, 106). Examples include:

- Affinity bias is the tendency to favour people who are like us in some way. When we gravitate toward people who are like ourselves, we may pay less attention to the people who are not as much like us. This can be a problem if we alienate the people who seem to be less like us and give the impression that we do not value their opinion as highly. Additionally, if we tend to solicit input just from the people who are most like us, we miss opportunities to gain new insights and diverse perspectives.
- Anchoring bias refers to making decisions from the first piece of information that we learn from.
- Confirmation bias can reinforce this as once we believe something to be true, we see more evidence that supports it.
- Negativity bias is when our minds react more strongly to negative experiences rather than positive ones, making us more likely to turn down opportunities or new ideas or new people as threats and not consider the potential advantages.

- Reactance bias occurs when we are forbidden to do something and then have the desire to do that exact thing in order to prove our freedom of choice.
- Frequency illusion – Have you noticed that when you learn a new word you start seeing it everywhere? Our brains have a habit of trying to see patterns, so we notice things more if they are interesting to us.

There are many more examples of such unconscious ways our brains work and as all brains function differently, different people lean more towards different biases. The question is where do they come from and what can we do about them?

Unconscious bias relates to the **mental "shortcuts"** our brain takes based on personal experiences and **stereotypes**. So, unconscious biases are the automatic, mental shortcuts used to process information and make decisions quickly. At any given moment individuals are flooded with information yet can only consciously process about 40 items. Cognitive filters and heuristics allow the mind to unconsciously prioritize, generalize, and dismiss large volumes of input. These shortcuts can be useful when making decisions with limited information, focus, or time, but can sometimes lead individuals astray and have unintended consequences in the workplace, overlook great ideas, undermine individual potential, as well as create a less than ideal work experience for other colleagues. Scientists have shown that such stereotypes begin to form early in childhood to serve a purpose for simplification. Clustering people into groups with expected traits does help navigate the world without being overwhelmed by information. The downside is that the potential for prejudice is hard-wired into human cognition. However, at the individual level, the extent to which such biases are internalised and acted on varies widely and in complex ways. It is therefore important to know that background, personal experiences, societal stereotypes and cultural context can have an impact on decisions and actions without realising it.

Yet it gets worse…. Even when we believe we are being rational in our thinking, we can still be misled. Attempts to observe others and their behaviour, free from any interpretation, can be hindered by observational errors. Judgement based on first impression still prevails. We are also prone to logical mistakes such as assuming people who speak well have deep thoughts. Stereotypes also play a part in our quick assumptions and the halo effect is the tendency for an impression created in one area to influence opinion in another area – essentially, overall impression of a person ("He is nice!") impacts evaluations of that person's specific traits ("He is also smart!").

Vivian Zayas, a professor of psychology at Cornell University, New York, and colleagues found that people continue to be influenced by another person's appearance even after interacting with them face-to-face (107). Their research found a strong consistency between how people evaluate others based on images, such as photographs and when they later meet in live interactions. Positive or negative, the original judgement remained after they meet. Professor Zayas has two explanations for the findings: Behavioural confirmation or self-fulfilling prophecy – observers look for information which confirm expectations, for example, those who had said they liked a person in a photograph tended to interact with them face to face in a friendlier, more engaged way. This is then picked up or responded to in kind, so it is reinforced. Secondly, regarding why people show consistency in judgments of personality, relates to the halo effect. People giving a photographed person a positive evaluation attributed other positive characteristics to them as well, such as linking attractiveness with social competence. In further studies, Zayas found that participants say they would revise their judgment of people in photographs if they had the chance to meet them in person, because they'd have more information on which to base their assessment. Yet results show that despite people thinking they would revise judgements people demonstrate little evidence of revision!

So, what does all this mean for leaders? What are important first and lasting impressions then? In the business context, professionalism counts, as it is about demonstrating skills and competencies for doing the job well. When asked what is associated with **professionalism**, appearance ranks second only to communication skills. Matthew Randall, the executive director of the Centre for Professional Excellence at York College of Pennsylvania, USA, who conducted polls in 2010 explained "how an individual dresses for work can be a powerful extension of personal brand. Clothes, accessories and even the footwear an employee chooses to wear help to reinforce or diminish their skills and qualities in the eyes of their employer, co-workers and clients" (108).

Again, how does this matter? For leaders, the critical link is to building respect. In his book "Winners, and how they succeed" Alistair Campbell examined sports stars, politicians and leaders, including how they built great teams (109). What he found was differing styles, but the common factor was that they were respected. For example, when interviewed, Clive Woodward, successful sports coach, was asked if he had to choose between being respected or liked by his players, Woodward responded, "I would go for respect every time". **Professional respect** is a feeling of deep admiration for someone elicited by their abilities, qualities, or achievements, not for looking cool or being liked, and should be the goal of leaders.

Personal Brand from Image to Impact

Businesses invest and manage brands as they create mental associations. Brands create expectations of the product or company and can be described as the promises the supplier is making towards a customer. Customers build trust in brands they experience or believe in and are willing to try new products just because of this trust. This is also true of people and as such, leaders especially need to consider their own personal brand and how they are perceived. If we accept that current social norms still require a dress code for business, we will explore how this, and other elements, can be combined to create a positive impression and a well "managed" personal brand.

Personal branding is establishing an impression in the minds of others. It is a managed process starting from building a professional business persona and delivered consistently throughout a career. It is creating a mark that identifies you and your career and one to use to express values, personality and skills. Since first described in 1997 by Tom Peters (110), the concept and value of personal branding has come a long way.

To define and manage personal brand it is important to understand personal drivers, then attempt to construct a narrative or description, then demonstrate it consistently in six ways:

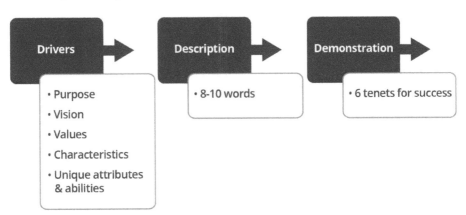

Figure 33: Steps for Defining a Personal Brand

Going back to self-awareness, consider the following:

- What is your purpose or passion?
- What is your vision for the future or career goals?
- What are your values you wish to promote?
- What characteristics describe you?

- What are your unique attributes and abilities, in other words where can you be seen as a credible, knowledgeable expert?

From these inputs, it is about describing a brand in 8-10 words.

Let's look at examples.

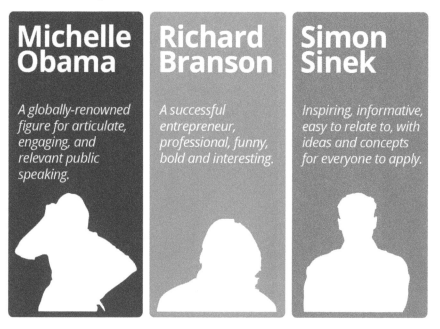

Figure 34: Examples of Strong Personal Brands (111)

Michelle Obama soared into the public eye during her time in office as first lady of USA. Far more than just the wife of the president, this incredible woman established herself as a thought-leader in her own right. The result is a brand that's known throughout the world. Michelle Obama is a globally-renowned figure for articulate, engaging, and relevant public speaking.

The founder of the Virgin Group, Richard Branson, is a great example of personal branding done right. He shows his personality in every aspect of his presence, allowing the crucial elements of what makes him unique to shine through. Branson has defined himself as a professional, but he's also showing people that he's funny, bold, and interesting too.

Demonstrating personal brand can also mean being able to describe who you are, what you can do for people and how you're going to do it. One of the best examples is Simon Sinek. From his personal website, to his social media pages, Sinek isn't just inspiring, he's informative too. Everything he does is well-designed and easy to relate to, so that you can instantly see what this professional is all about.

Inspired? You can have a go! Define your brand and consider how you would successfully demonstrate it consistently through **the six tenets**:

1. Performance and delivery of business results is always the foundation – deliver what you promise, over deliver in your role and contribute to business success

2. Leadership style or how you behave as a manager or team leaders also makes a difference – the extended transformational leadership model really is highly effective for building trust, engaging people and managing complex businesses of today.

Points 3 to 6, first impressions, dressing for success, speech and narrative, and body language, are specifically linked to building a professional business persona and as such, we will consider these further.

3. First impressions – In critical first meetings, such as interview situations, making a good and memorable first impression is key, and it happens in the first 7 seconds (100). So, remember to:

Smile – Facial expression says more about you than words. Make sure it's real and warm, confident and professional.

Shake hands – The handshake is the universally accepted signal of professionalism, politeness and confidence. A good handshake is a fine art; a tricky balance between a tight squeeze and a limp stroke. Additionally, if there are several people in the meeting, greet them all separately.

Introduce yourself – Never assume everyone knows who you are, so when you shake hands also say your name.

Speak clearly – Speak in a competent and confident way making sure what you say is relevant and appropriate. Speak slowly and talk at an appropriate pitch – people take others more seriously if you have a deeper voice.

Maintain eye contact – People are perceived as nervous or rude when they don't make eye contact. Therefore, to make a good first impression, make sure you lock eyes for at least three seconds at a time.

Look smart – We are judged on appearance in these seven seconds, so make sure there is nothing that could hinder the first impression. People continue to be influenced by another person's appearance even after interacting with them for significant time or when they have gathered additional information, as this is where behavioural confirmation bias keeps going and reinforces what we already believe to be correct.

4. Dressing for success with appropriate business attire – As said, the impressions individuals give to others greatly influence how they are viewed and treated at work

(100). Business attire has changed significantly over recent years, yet too many people have forgotten why proper business attire is still important. Though some companies encourage employees to dress casually, others require a more defined and professional dress code to maintain a professional image of the business, especially where employees routinely interact with clients and partners. Conflicts arise when employees dress for comfort or style, rather than realizing the importance of presenting themselves in a more professional manner. Yes, old-fashioned versus t-shirt-wearing Mark Zuckerberg, yet those wishing to build impact and reputation must be cognitive of the biases, prejudices and stereotypes linking appearance and competency.

If you wish to be taken seriously, dress for it. Dress for the next level, dress for the role you wish. You are unlikely to appear over dressed, rather, seen as a contender. Even if it says Business Casual, always wear a business suit. Especially as a woman in the business world, being absolutely professional at all times includes dress code. It is about adjusting for the situation – it is work, not home life or party time! Even for hairstyles, the key is to look professional again, not beautiful. So maybe it's a bit boring, but no experiments. Same is true for makeup – keep it simple. Jewellery also matters – it finishes off an outfit. And if you want a splash of colour, try a scarf. If it's the same colour as your eyes, it also draws attention to them. And as for stockings or tights. YES! You would laugh if a business man was not wearing socks so cover legs at all times.

Want an example? What comes to mind when you think about Angela Merkel? Successful politician? Well respected? Fashion icon?

Figure 35: **Angela Merkel: An Example of Dressing for Success**

You may be surprised to know that she travels with a stylist in her entourage, who's task it is to make sure the Merkel look is unchanged – same hair, same makeup, same style. She has a wardrobe of different-coloured jacket and trousers of the same design. It is a deliberate tactic to avoid comment on how she looks rather than inspire and it reinforces her personal brand of strategic seriousness (109).

5. Speech and narrative considers what you say and how you say it as this is also linked to personal brand and supports first impressions, good or bad. Communication skills are linked to professionalism and building trust (95) and a key competency (57) for employees and managers alike as mentioned. The goal of communication is not only to inform, but to engage others and build rapport. Beyond speaking clearly, in a competent and confident manner, make sure what you say is relevant and appropriate for the audience, avoiding slang and jargon. Speak slowly, at an appropriate pitch and set a positive tone. When talking to people one to one, show appreciation and ask questions. Genuine dialogue occurs when listening to understand, not listening to interrupt, with the intention of establishing a mutual relationship (86).

For leaders, it is also essential to go beyond the communication of tasks to being able to communicate a positive personal narrative (62). Part of who we are is knowing what our story is, giving a sense of identity, hence linked to brand. Considering brand drivers and brand description, this can create a narrative to explain where a leader or manager comes from and how this has shaped them, what they stand for, their values and their vision, and what they bring to the organization. Having the confidence to vocalise who we are may unconsciously influence us to act in a positive way and enable us to think about ourselves in an objective way.

Think about this as a personal pitch or a one-minute elevator speech; it has to be positive and simple, starting with a captivating headline, explaining why someone should listen based on the opportunity you bring and challenges you can overcome for them and what outcome will result. All too often we get bogged down with too many details on what we do and how we do it. Learning from Simon Sinek, again he advocates focusing on the "why" to inspire others (112). Learning to tell a story briefly also makes more impact. In "Brief", Joseph McCormack explains that as the average attention span is now down to 8 seconds, focused, concise messages are essential to overcome inattention and remain compelling (113).

6. Body language – Finally, it does not matter what you say unless it is augmented with appropriate accompanying body language. Our receptiveness to others, based on their words, is only 7%. Tone of voice is 38% and body language is 55%, including posture, gestures and eye contact (114).

Simple positive signals include a real smile, good eye contact, leaning in towards someone, using reaffirming noises and active participation in conversation. All shows warmth and genuine engagement. Signals of losing attention can include broken eye contact, turning away at 45-90°, slouching, checking a watch or even sighing. Defensive signals are arms crossed, leaning backwards and a blank face. Further disagreement signals include a set jaw, shaking head sideways and narrowed eyes.

To fully understand how communication works or even how misunderstandings may come about, it is important to note that communication is based on meaning and interaction and is framed in a social and cultural context (94). Human communication involves verbal and non-verbal elements and to understand a message properly, both have to be considered (94). When the verbal / non-verbal don't match, this confuses people and makes it difficult to understand the message. Non-verbal communication is much stronger, more intuitive and more difficult to manipulate therefore must be considered for impressions and impact.

Furthermore, Stanford Professor Deborah Gruenfeld believes that body language is especially important in power and influence (115). Research shows that people posed in expansive postures feel more powerful, exhibit higher testosterone levels and have lower levels of the stress hormone cortisol — all characteristics of high-ranking social status. Making eye contact while talking, but feeling free to look away when others do, is called having a high "look-speak to look-listen ratio," which is also common for dominant members of groups. Yet power is not only demonstrated through body language but also by "filling the room" – making sure that when you enter a room people know that you are there. Taking ownership of the space around you, means spreading your stuff and claiming territory physically.

Ultimately, what we are talking about is presence, a quality that is a blend of image, competencies and interpersonal skills, that when combined well, send all the right signals. It is having the full package of strong personal brand, making it clearer for everyone else to know what you stand for. It's a "wow" factor that sets people apart and gives a career that extra boost.

The Red Sneaker Effect

There are the likes of Mark Zuckerberg, CEO of Facebook, who, like many Millennials, prefers to dress in jeans and a T-shirt. Bucking the norms, Zuckerberg makes no effort to adhere to dress codes, rules and social norms to gain social acceptance and status (116). In his first-ever Q&A session, Mark Zuckerberg explained away his penchant for wearing grey T-shirts as a matter of efficient resource management, saying he does this to "clear my life so that I have to make as few decisions as possible about anything except how to best serve this (Facebook) community."

However, not only is this now a personal brand, there is evidence that this so-called "red sneakers effect" of non-conformity can confer higher status and competence, especially when it is intentional (117)! So, this may have worked for Zuckerberg and others pushing boundaries in high tech industries. However, as company founder Zuckerberg had more leeway than most of us are given, and though he has made it to chairman and CEO, even he conforms when the stakes are high. At the FaceBook AGM in May 2019, Zuckerberg could be seen donning the "uniform" of grey suit, white shirt and red tie as he attended for an important vote where he survived an attempt to make him step down as the company's chairman.

Key Learning Points

- Impressions individuals give to others greatly influence how they are viewed and treated at work: like it or not, our unconscious biases are extremely strong!

- First impressions seldom change therefore leaders should define and deliver a positive personal brand combining attitude, presence and ability, by managing performance, leadership style, first impressions, dressing for success, speech and narrative, and body language

- True and lasting influence comes from trust, power, understanding and personal presence – it is about relationships, hence connectedness with others and effective communication

- Beyond our relationships built over time, indirect influence is also conveyed through credibility and performance, meaning expertise, delivery and accountability

Personal Reflection Points

Question 1: Using a rating score of 1 to 10 with 1 being "could be much better" and 10 "excellent", how would you rate yourself for your current role for each of the elements that are important to achieving impact and influence:

I. Building trustful relationships through communication, positive environments, building coalitions and creating acceptance

II. Recognizing personal power and power structures, accessing resources through networks and motivating through shared vision and aligned goals

III. Understanding the interests of others, finding common ground, valuing diversity, engaging in genuine dialogue and seeking feedback

IV. Portraying a personal presence with a positive first impression and professional brand

Question 2: Does your rating suggest areas you need to work on, and if so, what will you do to improve?

Question 3: How do you believe you would rate for a more senior position? Would this impact your career planning?

Chapter 7
Becoming Transformational

Key Knowledge...

- The 5 Is of the extended Transformational Leadership model define qualities, behaviours and actions for highly effective leadership. The 1st I, idealized influence describes the anchors that begin with "self"

Key Actions...

- Serve as a role model
- Act authentically
- Create context to instil belonging and meaning
- Show integrity and ethical behaviour at all times

Impacts...

- Blueprint for bringing self to work
- Professional respect and admiration from others
- Creating a sustainable transformational environment where all can identify with organizational values and goals

Becoming transformational or developing a transformational leadership style is deeply rooted in self-awareness, self-regulation and self-development. The connectedness with self and the development of a personal brand identifies what is important. Demonstration of elements of **idealized influence** begins to show *how* a leader can go about it, and how to "show" a positive self, to influence the environment and people around in a positive way.

A Role Model by Leading with Influence and Emotional Intelligence

The reality for a leader is that their actions impact others every day. Leaders are looked upon for direction, guidance, even reassurance at times. The challenge is therefore showing a professional yet authentic persona in the context of managing tasks and people to achieve results. Idealized influence therefore starts with being **a role model** – a person others wish to emulate.

> *'A role model is a person who someone admires and whose behaviour they try to copy'*
>
> CAMBRIDGE DICTIONARY

Idealized influence was first described by Bass to mean a leader who demonstrated high ethical standards so could be counted on to do the right thing. They provide a vision, are trusted and respected by their team, and are strong role models (46). Initially, Bass named this first element "charisma", defining it as follows: "Charisma provides vision and sense of mission, instils pride, gains respect and trust" (46). However, later on, it was renamed idealized influence to mark the difference between transformational leadership and charismatic leadership. While charismatic leadership focuses on the personality of the leader, transformational leaders act as role models in order to empower and develop employees. While a charismatic leader may be admired by their team, the team remains dependent on them, identifies with the individual rather than the organization and will obey instructions without criticism. The risk is when such a leader leaves the organisation, the attached team may be unmotivated or unskilled to continue.

On the other hand, a transformational leader, who creates an environment where employees can develop and are empowered (67, 73), builds a team who identify with organizational values and goals, can self-organize and thereby have a more sustainable situation for the organization (119). In today´s business world, which is affected by constant and disruptive changes and multiple career changes, transformational leaders are therefore very valuable for organizations. This does not mean charisma does not count, but charisma alone is simply not enough to create a sustainable impact.

Acting as a role model is also required as transformational leaders set high expectations for their employees and this will only work, if the leaders themselves also live up to these expectations and understand the impact their own expectations and behaviours have on others. This links back to **emotional competencies** and the balance required for leadership. Ways to enhance emotional intelligence can include the following:

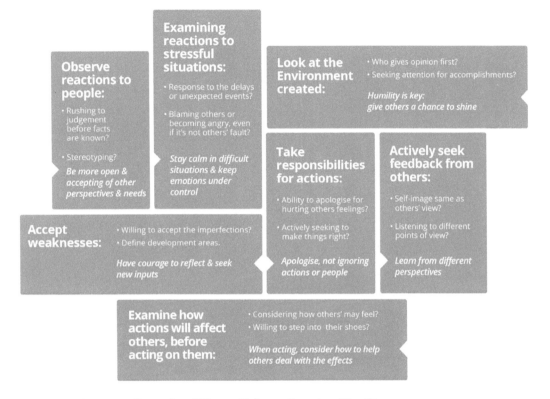

Figure 36: Examples of How to Enhance Emotional Intelligence

In addition to recent works on the importance of leaders with high emotional intelligence for decision making and building rapport (75, 76), emotional stability is also shown to be an important quality (120). Though some may thrive under positive pressure, those with well-developed emotional intelligence skills have the ability to behave consistently and never let their temper get out of control, even under challenging situations. The effects of emotional stability in leaders can be seen in:

- The team **performance**, including their commitment to company and results
- **Physical health** can also be impacted: Uncontrolled stress can lead to medical conditions, so learning how to relieve stress, to remain calm, show objectivity and not over-react is critical.
- Uncontrolled stress can also impact **mental health**, making people vulnerable to anxiety and depression. If unable to understand and manage emotions, leaders may appear irrational, inconsistent and "moody", reducing the ability to build trust and leaving them feeling isolated.

- Lastly, by understanding emotions and how to control them, leaders are better able to express how they feel and understand how others are feeling. This allows genuine empathetic dialogue and forging stronger **relationships** long term. For an employee, the experience is then one of being listened to, considered and included.

Creating influence also only works when others observe genuineness, commitment and integrity from a leader. With the challenges of business today and the need for adapting to people and situations, how can a leader stay true to themselves and be consistent and fair to all? The answer lies in a leader's ability to be authentic.

Acting Authentically

Much can be learnt from observing or reading about highly successful leaders such as these examples.

Figure 37: Example of Highly Successful Leaders

There are some characteristics they share, such as self-confidence and emotional stability. Their behaviours are highly focused on task and people for optimal engagement and productivity. They also adapt to people and situations for success. What they also do is demonstrate all the competencies of Transformational Leadership (5 Is). However, these leaders are not all the same. They still have a uniqueness in their approach based on a combination of their values, their experiences and how they reach out to others. By bringing these elements of self to work, they are showing an authenticity and a human quality to build trusting collaborations and influence others positively.

Being authentic, and finding a path to authenticity takes time, but yields strong results. In 2007, author Bill George, Harvard Business School professor and former chairman and CEO of Medtronic, conducted a large leadership development study that showed achieving good business results over a long period of time is indicative of authentic leadership (121). How leaders become and remain authentic includes:

- **Self-observation** and honestly defining personal needs, desires, strengths and weaknesses. From these, leaders can set goals and plans for improvement. However, as part of authenticity and transformational leadership, further probing into values and motives is required for alignment to company fit.

"Telling our personal story reveals the shape shifting landscape of our mind." Kilroy J. Oldster (122)

- **Continuous learning** because no one has all the answers. Curiosity and life-long learning define successful people who strive to be their best. This is not only seen in skills they develop, but also in how they think and approach new challenges. Such people can also be described as agile learners: Not afraid to admit they don't know it all, keen observers, those that look for comparisons, apply lateral thinking or guiding principles, can adapt, and keep learning from all situations.

"Ideas rarely come from doing nothing. We stimulate our brains to come up with ideas when we learn new things" Philippa Perry (62)

- **Integrating life into work** by using life experiences to find the inspiration to make an impact in the world. This includes drawing on formative events, both good and bad, to transform, to focus on what is personally important and build inner confidence. For example, Heather Schuck, US entrepreneur, built a $14 million dollar fashion empire from her kitchen table and then used her experiences of trying to balance work/life balance in her book "The Working Mom Manifesto" (123).

"You will never feel truly satisfied by work until you are satisfied by life" Heather Schuck (123)

- **Reaching out to others** because people need people and having a strong support network is essential for sanity and leadership success. Taking time to build and maintain a broad network from friends, family, colleagues and mentors not only provides perspective and new ideas, relating to others provides outlet for personal stress. The ability to receive support from good people also means leaders can cascade learning and development. Empowering other people to also step up and lead results in sustainable, long term success.

"Surround yourself with people who are going to lift you higher" Oprah Winfrey (124)

A word of caution – strong emphasis on "self" and using this as the foundation to build influence on others may risk lack of concern for the wishes or opinions of others. Leaders must be cognitive that they only see the world from their place. Leaders must never assume that other people see things the same way or value the same things. How people perceive events, messages and actions can be influenced by many factors including age, values, personality, gender, background, culture, beliefs, even how they are feeling today… (125). Though being authentic is a behavioural anchor in achieving idealised influence, transformational leadership also requires abilities associated with inter-personal elements that support needs and perspectives of others. Yet when authenticity is achieved it permits staying true to one's self, bringing a sense of self to the workplace and a sensitivity to reach out to others, thereby gaining trust.

Creating Context to Instil Belonging and Meaning

For a leader to step forward, and show the way, they need to believe in what they are doing and create context for others – it has to make sense. In other words, for a leader to behave authentically and ethically to lead others, staying true to personal values is critical. Especially in difficult times, disruptive change, restructuring and other examples of uncertainty, leaders are often required to deliver tough messages, reshape teams and even close business areas. The decision point is not whether to act or when, it is how a leader approaches the task and handles the individuals. This is when trust, respect and integrity count.

Not only do individuals have **values**, also companies do as part of **corporate culture** (12) and together with vision, mission and strategies, they form the identity of the company. As a leader, knowing the company story, focusing on goals and key projects, and believing in the company journey is essential and part of the role. As a leader, it is therefore important to consider if personal values and motives are aligned with their company's. Many would choose not to work for an oil company if the company exploited natural resources ruthlessly. Many may not wish to work for a hire and fire type organization that did not believe in its people. So, as a leader, you have to ask yourself, does this company behave in a way I am comfortable with?

Company identity is not only important for employees to find meaning and direction, identity is also crucial for peoples' decisions to join a specific company. When surveys ask what people look for when applying for jobs, the top 3 answers for

Millennials (Generation Y) are purpose, career development and atmosphere (126). To attract such talent, companies actively manage their image, as well as openly communicate business strategies, people strategies, culture and values. In this way, people can choose to join a company that will engage them. Studies also show that an engaged workforce is more motivated and productive because people take pride in what they are doing and have faith in those around them (127). This leads to better working relationships, greater collaboration and ultimately a more successful organisation. For example, winner of the UK Best Company 2018 was EE, the mobile telecommunications company. It won because of it values embedded through the organisation. All employees identified with the values which gave common language and focus for meeting goals.

> '*If employees are put to extraordinary efforts to realize company targets, they must be able to identify with them*'
>
> BARTLETT *ET AL* (8)

Many parts of corporate culture and identity are implicit, and people are not aware, therefore a leader's role is to translate meaning to others. The best leaders achieve this successfully and credibly when their own values are aligned and therefore their position and message is authentic. Successful companies have also been shown to hire senior leaders who share the corporate vision and values (128). A shared vision ensures business strategies and plans deliver on what the company wants to be and wants to achieve. Shared values drive how the company acts and become embedded in the policies and procedures established.

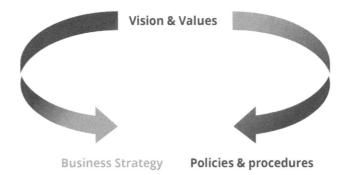

Figure 38: How Vision and Values Translate into Business Actions

The leadership challenge is using vision and values to create context for all employees. This requires communication, communication, communication, and emphasising values through daily actions and across all functions, to create a positive culture. For example, hiring for values, role modelling and rewarding them and avoiding any misalignment, as misalignment can be demotivating. Finally, aligning all projects and activities with the strategic focus, thereby adding to business performance.

Integrity and Ethical Behaviour

This is the final anchor of idealized influence and the connection is building **trust**. Why is trust so important in business? Think about your own experiences: how does it feel to work together with a person you trust, as compared to working with a person you do not trust? It makes a huge difference, and not only in business environments, as trust is the "lifeblood of all healthy relationships" (129). As discussed in depth in chapter 6, trust is one of the three core elements of influence, influencing the relationship between two people.

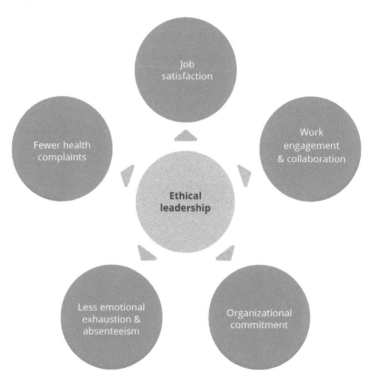

Figure 39: **Examples of Positive Effects of Ethical Leadership**

Ethics also count in business as shown when companies face scandals due to corruption for example. When leaders don't follow ethical standards, the result can be loss of reputation, loss of money and legal consequences. For a business, it is not only about preventing unethical behaviour. Many studies have shown that there are benefits if leaders and decision makers behave ethically (92, 130, 131).

Most positive effects can be measured on employee engagement – if working in an ethical environment, job satisfaction, work engagement as well as levels of collaboration are increased. There is also greater organizational commitment, and at the same time, ethical behaviour minimizes the emotional exhaustion, absenteeism and health problems of their employees.

Finally, **trustworthiness** is an outcome of ethical behaviour (132). To build a trusted reputation this means defining the expectations and then adhering to these and consistently demonstrating them by being honest and showing integrity, concern for others and fairness – doing the right thing for the business and people at all times. Yet trust is also required in all directions. Trusting others around you means empowering others, delegating responsibility for decision making for example, and supporting and accepting failure in the process. By defining and adhering to ethical standards for themselves and their team, leaders can create solid, two-way trust, necessary for engagement and long-term business success.

In summary, the first I of the **extended Transformational Leadership model**, "idealized influence" goes beyond key knowledge and considers *how* to achieve connectedness with "self" and to bring this to the work place. To bring this concept further to life, here are examples of actions from highly successful global leaders.

What Idealized Influence Looks Like in Practice

"When you want people to show passion, then you have to show it yourself". *Peer M. Schatz.*

"When I look around, it is the leaders who remain humble that stand out as it's a prerequisite for self-reflection, learning, listening, breaking silos and being authentic". *Natacha Piekatz-Hausammann, Vice President Inside Sales EMEA.*

"To be a role model to my team it is about the small things. I always make sure that I attend meetings on time and not have the team wait for me. It is important to demonstrate behaviour I expect and show respect for my teams' time. It is also about being available for my team, being there when they need me, having a real open door!". *Thomas Schweins, Senior Vice President, QIAGEN.*

"The more senior a role you hold, the less feedback you receive. It means effort is required to ask for true feedback, yet this is essential for growth." *Peer M. Schatz.*

"Being a leader is not all about delivering the great news! Acting authentically is critical when delivering a difficult message i.e. making some one redundant. Be sincere, honest and clear and you will gain respect. Empathise but be genuine and have clear outcomes in mind. This can be employed for general performance feed-back too!". *Alison Staley, HR Consultant and Chartered Fellow of Chartered Institute of Personnel and Development.*

"If you want ethical behaviour in the workplace there has to be consequences for anyone working against the defined standards". *Peer M. Schatz.*

"As part of ethical business behaviour, leaders need to show "managerial courage" and by that, I mean doing the right thing for the business, making the difficult decisions and taking responsibility for outcomes". *Natacha Piekatz-Hausammann, Vice President Inside Sales EMEA.*

Key Learning Points

- Leadership starts from self and exceptional leaders have the courage to bring "self" to work by acting as role models, showing authenticity, sharing values, setting direction for others, and always showing integrity. It is their ability to shift beyond ego to purpose and act with humility and respect for all others

- Strong emotional intelligence and emotional stability once again provide the foundation for strong relationships, team performance and health

- Authenticity also requires self-observation, learning, integrating life into work and choosing to reach out to others

- Personal values must match organizational values to believe in what we are doing

- Leaders must be able to live and share the organizational story from vision and strategy to team goals and daily tasks

- Setting high performance and ethical standards can inspire and raise the bar for others as long as leaders also live up to them

Personal Reflection Points

Question 1: Can you use curiosity, courage and kindness for greater good as a leader? Ask yourself:

What would I be asking if I was more curious about what I did and how it was impacting others?

What would I do if I was more courageous about acting authentically?

What would my decision regarding situations look like if kindness was driving the decision?

Question 2: How do you share your personal story?

What personal values do you communicate with others and why?

Do you have a vision for your leadership style?

How do you demonstrate trust?

How to Connect with Others in the Digital Age

Welcome to Part Three, our deep dive into how best to connect with others using the extended transformational leadership model as a guide. In chapter 7 we considered idealized influence as part of "self". Here we will look at the remaining four of the five Is as they relate to others.

Competences of Extended Transformational Leadership (5 Is) in the Digital Age:

A model to create an environment of trust, based around connecting with self and others.

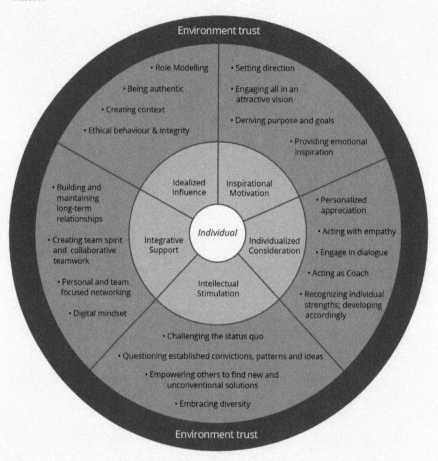

Figure 40: The Competencies of the Extended Transformational Leadership Model

Chapter 8

Bringing Others on the Journey

Key Knowledge...

- The 2nd I, inspirational motivation, describes how to set direction for others

Key Actions...

- Engage others in an attractive vision
- Leverage purpose and achievement as motivators
- Set meaningful goals with others to drive performance
- Provide emotional connection by speaking to inspire others

Impacts...

- When employees are committed to a vision, their actions will be aligned to achieve it and their satisfaction, motivation and performance increases
- When employees understand the impact, their contribution has to the whole, the more engaged they are in delivering organizational success
- Understanding the reason" why" we do what we do (purpose), combined with difficult and specific goals is motivational and people work harder to achieve
- Motivators can be highly individual, yet common factors exist and can be leveraged by all leaders

Inspirational motivation is the second of the five I's of extended Transformation Leadership and in this context, it is the role of the leader to create an environment in which everyone can succeed. This begins by inspiring others to want to believe in the organizational direction. It is winning hearts and minds and ensuring everyone is on the same journey plan. To achieve this, a leader needs to be able to show others a new horizon or new ideas that will provide momentum for actions. It is about setting a direction that others also want to strive for. This means having a clear picture of the future, a vision, and bringing the team on board and connecting them to this vision.

Engaging Others in an Attractive Vision

A vision describes the long term aims and direction of a company. Companies then use strategic plans to achieve shorter term milestones or goals, to ultimately achieve future goals and vision.

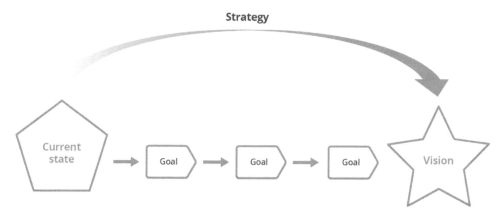

Figure 41: How Vision Marks Future Direction

As such, visions are positive, emotionally charged images of a desirable, and at the same time, an achievable future for individuals, groups or organizations (133). This differs from a mission, which defines the reason for the organization. Whereas a company mission describes what a business does today, a vision describes what they hope to accomplish by executing on that mission. When also combined with company values, the full purpose of the organization becomes clearer and thereby directing and aligning the actions of all employees. As John F Kennedy said, "efforts and courage are not enough without purpose and direction" (134).

'It is fine to stress what to aim for but people also need to know what the company stands for'

BARTLETT *ET AL* (8)

Leadership studies have consistently acknowledged the essence of a vision as a significant component and prerequisite of leadership performance. A vision is not only the description of where we want to be in the future, a good vision that creates a mental picture also has access to unconscious needs and motivators (133), therefore has the power to inspire and direct actions. A vision can also be considered a compass, aligning efforts and focusing on significant goals. Visions also answer big questions on why we care or bother, in other words, engaging people in what they do and why they do it. Through engagement, direct impact can also be measured financially.

In an example, Best Buy claimed better employee engagement drove increased operating income and profitability. They reported that a 0.1 % increase in employee engagement drove $100,000 in operating income to the bottom line of each store per year (135).

A vision statement describes not only where the company wants to be or achieve long term, it can also include the community or the world it wishes to have as a result of the company's services. It can also be an evolution over time as a company develops. For example, when Microsoft was founded, Bill Gates dreamed of "a computer on every desk and in every home" and today the company vision is "to help people and businesses throughout the world realize their full potential".

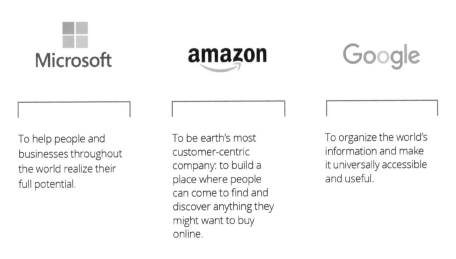

To help people and businesses throughout the world realize their full potential.

To be earth's most customer-centric company: to build a place where people can come to find and discover anything they might want to buy online.

To organize the world's information and make it universally accessible and useful.

Figure 42: Examples of Company Visions

Amazon state "Our vision is to be earth's most customer-centric company; to build a place where people can come to find and discover anything they might want to buy online." And for GOOGLE, their vision is "To organize the world's information and make it universally accessible and useful." All of these can be considered very big dreams, yet they guide all strategies and actions for these companies and set out clear long-term intent.

Crafting a Team or Project Vision

Visions allow employees and teams to orientate and focus through meaning and motivation. Visions can be defined for an organization and they can also be defined for a team or a project or a change scenario. The question for a leader would be how it should be formulated. Firstly, it must be in line with the organizations' corporate vision. Secondly to be effective, Kotter's 6 characteristics outline this well (136):

Imaginable – The people who consume the vision must be able to paint a rational picture in their mind of what the world will be like if the vision is attained.

Desirable – The vision appeals to the long-term interests of those being asked to act.

Feasible – The vision has to be attainable.

Focused – The vision provides enough clarity and alignment to guide organizational decisions.

Flexible – The vision must provide enough direction to guide but not enough to restrict individual initiative.

Communicable – The vision must be consumable and understandable to everyone involved.

A leader who shows passion in their work can be considered one that is able to demonstrate the first I, idealized influence. An aim of the second I, inspiration motivation is spreading this passion to others to achieve greater reach – a domino effect if you like – impacting more people and driving more actions in the organization. One way to achieve such an effect is by involving people. Hence involving teams in formulating a vision means they feel committed. With it, commitment brings dedication to the vision and actions to achieve it. When teams have a say in how successful the organization can become and this leads to higher satisfaction, motivation and overall better performance (18). This must be an active process though where expertise is sought, conventions and cross-functional boundaries ignored and there is an openness to contributions from all. Especially in a group setting, a leader must ask for inputs, not simply giving their opinion. They must specifically direct questions at quieter team members to avoid loss of all perspectives and they must challenge given statements and norms to ensure new ideas surface.

*'Nobody plays the game from the side-lines. Every-
one has to be invested in the outcome, and the only
way to do that is to put everyone into the game'*

BRECHTER (137)

What Happens When Vision is Missing?

When vision is missing, confusion occurs (138). On the other hand, chaos from lack of focus can be caused by a poor vision or one that is simply not communicated well. Kotter also suggested that if a vision can't be explained in five minutes it has failed the test of being communicable (136). This highlights that formulating the vision plays only a minor role in being a transformational leader. What´s really important is what happens with the vision! If it is simply written on the wall but never referred to or acted upon, the vision is worth nothing. So, it is crucial that a vision is communicated properly and converted into action!

This means communication must be relevant to the audience – why they should listen, what it means to them, and what is expected of them in terms of actions and next steps. And because visions have the power to inspire, any communication around them should be designed to excite, paint a picture, engage imaginations, make people dream…. The message should also be repeated to maintain direction and focus over time, never a one off, more an instrument to guide a company even when the day to day means delving into tasks and details. Finally, vision should be visible across the organization, in all strategies and plans created to deliver the vision (128).

When it's done right, the impact of an inspiring vision can be seen not only in achievement itself, but also by the feelings instilled in a nation and in generations to come.

"We choose to go to the moon. We choose to go to the moon in this decade and do the other things, not because they are easy, but because they are hard, because that goal will serve to organize and measure the best of our energies and skills, because that challenge is one that we are willing to accept, one we are unwilling to postpone, and one which we intend to win…" (139)

These words from John F Kennedy, in 1962, are considered one of the best examples of inspirational motivation – showing a future dream, a journey of courage, a challenge and direction for NASA, way beyond the first manned lunar landing in July 1969.

Leveraging Purpose and Achievement as Motivators

To achieve inspirational motivation, a leader needs to show others a new horizon through a vision, and secondly, this bigger picture needs to be translated to individuals, their work and their tasks. So overall, it is about setting a direction that others want to strive for and showing them how to get there. The challenge for a leader is understanding what is motivating for each individual and how to use this to engage them.

As mentioned in chapter 1, American psychologist David McClelland, described the needs we all have for achievement, affiliation, and power. Individuals will have different characteristics depending on their dominant motivator (23).

Achievement is the strong need to set and accomplish challenging goals, take calculated risks and receive regular feedback on progress and achievements.

Affiliation wants to belong to the group, favouring collaboration over competition and not liking high risk or uncertainty.

Power is linked to control and influencing others, winning and enjoying status and recognition. Those with a strong power motivator are divided into two groups: personal and institutional. People with a personal power drive want to control others, while people with an institutional power drive like to organize the efforts of a team to further the company's goals.

Understanding motivational theory and intrinsic motivators is one thing, yet as a transformational leader, knowing how to motivate and bring out the best in each individual, is required. To do this, spending time finding out what motivates employees is essential. Only then can a leader provide tasks or opportunities which will really motivate each person and enable each to succeed. For example, being given a challenging task can be very motivating for one person, while another colleague could be overwhelmed by it.

'Everyone is a genius. But if you judge a fish on its ability to climb a tree, it will live its whole life believing it is stupid'

ALBERT EINSTEIN (140)

Factors That Motivate and Engage People

From a full review of multiple research studies and our own experiences, we have found that not only do people want to succeed personally and have personal motivations, there are common factors that leaders can leverage within teams.

Figure 43: Common Factors that Motivate People at Work

People are more motivated and engaged in a company that is successful, so a winning company, with a strong reputation is an essential starting point. Opportunities for expansion and growth, including learning through training, coaching and feedback, are also key. Career advancement is a motivator, especially seen in Millennials, expecting challenging projects, and fast progression with defined career steps. Global community, access to international networks and social interactions are also important.

Core company values are associated with engagement, meaning productivity, pride and faith in others (6, 7, 8). These include benefits policies such as fair pay, recognition for performance, health support and flexible provisions. The working environment too can be a motivator when the atmosphere is friendly and fun, offices are in good locations and personal time management is supported with flexible arrangements for work / life balance. In addition, being inspired by leaders, the leadership style, the relationship with leaders, access to leaders and confidence in leaders are also considered motivating. Lastly, a sense of purpose is highly motivating and as such will be considered in more detail.

*'Passion and purpose are better compass
needles for life than job titles'*

KATHRYN SULLIVAN (141)

Looking more deeply at **purpose**, studies have shown that this is the top reason Millennials join a company (126). It is based on a desire to work for a company that can change the world for a better place. Purpose is understanding the reason" why". As a leader, conveying purpose comes from framing the company story through communication. It is translating (8) the corporate vision and values into every-day roles, responsibilities, projects, goals, plans and policies. It is assigning meaningful jobs and tasks and recognizing the value of the work each individual does and how this contributes to the overall success of the company. It is also about celebrating the **achievements**.

The benefits of a purpose-driven culture mean less control, less short termism and more emphasis on inspiring people to give the best of themselves every day (128).

*'Profit isn't a purpose, it's a result. To have purpose
means the things we do are of real value to others'*

SIMON SINEK (112)

Setting Goals as Performance Drivers

Goal setting involves the development of an action plan designed specifically to motivate and guide a person or team. In the late 1960s, Locke pioneered research into goal setting and motivation and showed that clear goals and appropriate feedback motivate employees and in turn, improves performance (142). The more difficult and specific a goal is, the harder people tend to work to achieve it. Likewise, having a goal that's too easy is not motivating.

And if there are no goals, there is loss of purpose and not much fun. Imagine a football match without goal posts, hiking without a final destination, a wedding without a ceremony. All of these events lose their purpose.

According to Locke *et al*, there are five **goal setting principles** that can improve chances of success:

- Clarity – such as defined SMART goals
- Challenge – stretching yet achievable goals
- Commitment – occurs when teams understand and agree to the goals and are therefore more likely to "buy in" if they have been involved in goal setting
- Feedback – involves listening, assessing progression and adjusting difficulty levels if required
- Task complexity – means taking care to ensure work doesn't become too overwhelming when goals or assignments are highly complex – leaders who work in complicated and demanding roles often push themselves hard and risk doing so to others if they don't take account of the complexity of the task for others.

All managers have to set goals for themselves and others to ensure team tasks contribute to organizational success. It is an essential management competency to break down corporate goals to individual goals, ensuring all actions are in alignment with the company´s vision and strategy. This focus on so called "**Performance Management**" must also measure individual goal **achievement**, yet broader than assigning responsibilities and tasks, it is showing how every individual contributes to the success of the whole organization, and motivates though achievement and delivery of personal, team and corporate goals.

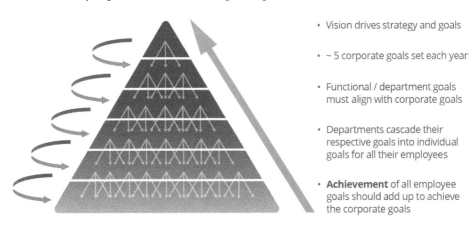

- Vision drives strategy and goals

- ~ 5 corporate goals set each year

- Functional / department goals must align with corporate goals

- Departments cascade their respective goals into individual goals for all their employees

- **Achievement** of all employee goals should add up to achieve the corporate goals

Figure 44: How Goals Cascade from Vision and Back

As Burns (45) and Bass (46, 53) also stated, a transformational leader provides inspiration motivation by creating common pictures (vision) and communicating high expectations to employees (goals). Critically, the entire process and communication of goals and results should be transparent for real impact.

Money? Let's consider the topic of money as a motivator. Believe it or not – money is proven not to be a motivator (143). Yes, employees are happy about a pay raise for a short time, yet it does not motivate them sustainably. Mid- and long-term, the impact of a salary change or bonus decreases, because the higher salary level becomes the new norm. This means that pay can be considered a "hygiene factor".

In the 1950s, American psychologist Frederick Herzberg identified different motivational factors and classified them into two categories: **hygiene factors and motivators** (144). The hygiene factors need to be taken care of in order to prevent demotivation and to set the base for motivation, yet they will not lead to motivation on their own. For example, ensuring that all employees have a working computer prevents demotivation, but only the fact of having a computer that works does not motivate.

Figure 45: Examples of Herzberg's Hygiene Factors and Motivators

True motivation only arises from fulfilling the motivators, for example recognition. Also, work itself and the possibility of mastering new tasks can be motivators according to Herzberg.

When considering money in this light, salary has to be maintained in order to prevent demotivation, but it does not lead to positive motivation. Other research even goes a step further – in many cases, monetary rewards can even decrease motivation (145, 146)! Renowned psychology professor Edward Deci stated human beings have an "inherent tendency to seek out novelty and challenges, to extend and exercise their capacities, to explore, and to learn. When money is used as an external reward for some activity, the subjects lose intrinsic interest for the activity."

The essence of transformational leadership is the "ability of the leader to transfer inspiring goals and gain the trust of employees to lead them to performance that reached beyond the limits of their own imagination" (67). Here, the leader must enable the performance and success of individuals by framing their roles in terms of overall direction, purpose and goals of the organization. This has to also be in the context of ability to act, hence augmented by individual development, and lastly requires the individuals' own responsibility and commitment to the organization's success. This is how leaders enable all individuals to succeed in their role:

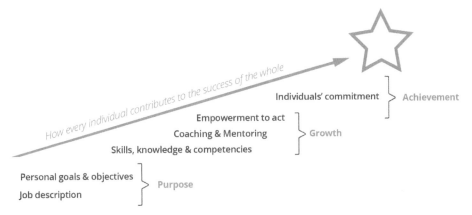

Figure 46: How Leaders Can Enable All Individuals to Succeed

Providing Emotional Connection by Speaking to Inspire

For a transformational leader to motivate individuals and inspire teams, they not only have to have the ability to set a future direction and utilize a sense of purpose and set effective goals, they also need the ability tell the organizational story in a way that captures imaginations and influences employees. It is the broader winning of hearts and minds, such that all want to work harder for the common goal. For the leader it once again comes down to effective communication!

'Good communication is as stimulating as black coffee, and just as hard to sleep after'

ANNE MORROW LINDBERGH (147)

Communication as a Meta-Competency

We refer to effective communication in every aspect of leadership: Simply put, leadership *is* communication as it is how we convey meaning to others. As mentioned in chapter 3, effective communication is also considered a meta-competency (56, 57), an overarching ability, relevant to a wide range of work settings and which facilitates adaptation and flexibility, for success with others. Our communication style is critical because it is how we come across to others, linked with first impressions we give, and is conscious behaviour based on how we choose to motivate and influence others, and as such, impacts employee engagement. As a competency it includes abilities to:

- Think with clarity
- Express ideas, facts and information consistently
- Choose appropriate language a multitude of differing audience types will best understand
- Handle the rapid flows of information within the organization, and among customers, partners, and other stakeholders and influencers
- Handle discrepancies and conflicts in a constructive manner
- Skills to support such outcomes include listening, engaging others in dialogue, utilizing ideas from others, facilitating meetings, summarizing discussions, actively distributing clear information, presenting concepts and facts, and inspiring emotionally

There is much evidence that communicating in an inspiring way increases effectiveness as a leader, and as people become more engaged, their levels of achievement and their sense of common purpose and well-being rise (148). To quote Simon Sinek, "there are leaders and there are those who lead. Leaders hold a position of power or influence, but those who lead inspire us. Whether they are individuals or organizations, we follow those who lead, not because we have to, but because we want to. We follow those who lead, not for them, but for ourselves. And it's those who start with "why" that have the ability to inspire those around them" (112). Sinek refers to "The Golden Circle" of communication starting with why, including why organizations do what they do – the purpose – the reason the organization exists, before talking what and how.

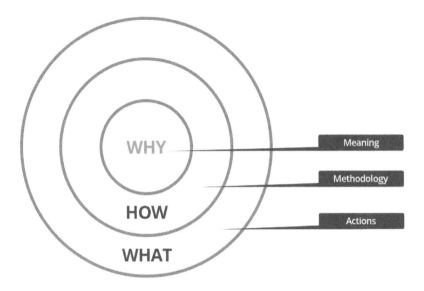

Figure 47: Representation of the Golden Circle Starting with Why

The challenge however is that most work communication, especially in groups, is detailed and operational, focused on what to do, how to do, who does it by when etc. Though important, this is not the inspiring part. To engage people on a more emotional level, the message must explain the WHY first (87). There are two forces that govern human behaviour, why and how. Why is the motive for doing something, the meaning. How is the method of doing it, the part that is objective and detailed. When it comes to engagement and buy-in, motive trumps method, in other words, why trumps how. Easier said than done though as how is simpler and less stressful to talk about in many situations.

How to Take Communication to a Deeper Level

1. Firstly, the core message must explain WHY.
2. To create a sense of feeling, the tone of a message is important. People expect leaders to convey optimism and confidence, share common purpose or values and express their personal commitment.
3. Balanced facts give credibility to a message. An honest presentation of positive and negative information for example, upsides and downsides. A focus on future orientation or an external view such as the customer perspective also adds weight and believability.
4. Any communication message should also include a what's next – what you want people to do now. Be specific on desired actions.

5. Use tools to make communication messages more memorable: Using images, not all text; telling stories to capture ideas and concepts; referring to other sources for evidence; engaging others in open questions for transparency
6. Lastly, keeping communication short and simple so not to overwhelm or bore. This goes back to influence and the concept of "Brief" (113) that we introduced in chapter 6.

It is one thing to say what you think is correct, however communication is not effective if people did not hear, understand or feel motivated to think differently and act differently as a result. Standing up and talking at people is not inspiring. Only when words have an impact is there success and people listen from behind their own filters – filters that may be cultural or emotional, or in place because of unique perceptions or even misunderstandings.

To inspire or elicit change, communication needs to be about their concerns, their issues. This is what is meant by leaders being audience-centric in communication, and to recognize that, when it comes to communication, it is all about the others.

For example, when communicating a vision, evidence indicates that people find two aspects of the vision motivating and inspiring (149):

1. When the vision and their work is meaningful to them as individuals
2. When these aspects are also sufficiently ambitious to be motivating, but not so challenging that they will be daunted by the prospect.

Beyond the why, individuals need information for buy-in or decision making. However, individuals make decisions in different ways and communicate differently as we discussed in chapter 5. By understanding other people, information can be tailored to their needs better. Ask yourself, what do they need from you to buy-in or make a decision in a timely manner?

A good leader therefore adapts their communication style depending on the person or audience. This requires that a leader should identify the audience and their characteristics and interests, then adjust the communication style based on what the audience needs and what will encourage them to react to meet the goals of the communication. Throughout a day, a leader may have to switch between styles to ensure the right message is received in the right way.

It may well be obvious to plan and even practice communication for formal meetings and presentations, yet as a leader, a role model and someone others look to for guidance and support, it is essential to be professional and effective in all situations!

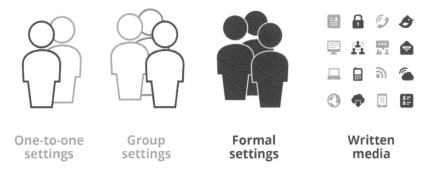

One-to-one   Group   **Formal**   **Written**
settings   settings   **settings**   **media**

Figure 48: Communication Scenarios

- *One-to-one*: when the leader must engage the other party, show empathy, use open questions, listen, integrate ideas and use appropriate body language
- *In Group settings*: skills here include actively leading discussions and facilitating outcomes, integrating all other members, summarizing, agreeing actions and defining next steps. It does not mean simply voicing your opinion to gain agreement.
- *In Formal presentations*: leaders must learn a professional yet authentic style which includes good body language, focus on key messages, clear structure, appropriate use of slides or tools, combined with enthusiasm and inspiration!
- Finally, in *written forms*, especially digital media with its long-life span, messages must be clear, avoid ambiguity and not open for misinterpretation. Today, with many leaders choosing to produce social media content, write blogs, use twitter etc, the opportunity to inspire via such channels is exciting, offering new levels of quality and timeliness of information.

The result of speaking to inspire is to build trust and team spirit, whilst also conveying identity with organizational vision and values. It is leveraging a common purpose to achieve pride and loyalty. When seen in this way, it can be seen that, "the art of communication is the language of leadership" to bring people on the journey" to quote James C Humes (150).

In summary, the second I of the **extended Transformational Leadership model**, "inspirational motivation" considers *how* to begin to connect with others and motivating others for a shared purpose. To bring this concept further to life, here are examples of actions from highly successful global leaders.

What Inspirational Motivation Looks Like in Practice

"To inspire and motivate my team I always make sure that goals and initiatives are defined by the team. This creates much more buy in than telling people what to do". *Thomas Schweins, Senior Vice President, QIAGEN.*

"For understanding the why, it is essential to make it explicit – what the company does and why everyone's contribution is important. I find the "Brief" methodology by Joseph McCormack an excellent tool for creating concise messages that people can follow." *Peer M. Schatz.*

"Crucial to driving through new strategies or new initiative is creating context. Context provides deeper knowledge and understanding in order to engage people. This means sharing and discussing as much as possible – what is the current state, why the new approach, what is the desired future state and what are the key steps and deliverables to reach the goal. Specifics are important to ensure your team are on the same journey with you." *Alison Staley, HR Consultant and Chartered Fellow of Chartered Institute of Personnel and Development.*

Key Learning Points

- Bringing others on the journey starts by setting direction
- Creating and communicating a desirable and achievable vision is highly motivating to others
- Lack of vision causes confusion
- Visions align efforts and focus in on significant goals
- Goals in themselves are motivating, they show people how to succeed and provide targets and purpose
- Achieving goals is also motivating and gives sense of reward and understanding of contributions to the organization
- Though motives can be very personal, common motivators include opportunities for expansion and growth, alignment with organizational values and purpose
- Money is not a motivator, it is a hygiene factor that must be taken care of fairly, alongside policies, physical environment and co-worker relationships
- How to engage others on the journey and inspire is linked to effective communication, starting from the "why", to connecting emotionally with people and being relevant and consistent at all times

Personal Reflection Points

Question 1: How do you inspire others and create purpose?

Question 2: How do you tell your organizational story?

Question 3: What is your personal and team vision?

Question 4: How do you motivate others as a team and as individuals?

Chapter 9

Treating People as Individuals

Key Knowledge...

- The 3rd I, individualized consideration, describes how to have strong people-orientation and approach others as valued individuals

Key Actions...

- Demonstrate personal appreciation for others and their work contributions
- Act with empathy and engage in genuine dialogue
- Act as coach for team members and colleagues alike
- Recognize individual strengths and develop accordingly

Impacts...

- Individuals are treated with care and compassion, creating an open and trusting culture
- Team members feel valued, appreciated and have clarity on how they contribute to the whole
- Team members become more confident, knowledgeable, self-directed and self-sufficient
- Teams are developed for personal growth and to meet future organizational goals

The opportunity stemming from an understanding of the uniqueness of transformational leadership is the central concept of individuality. This means seeing leadership as a process that occurs between employees and leaders, taking into consideration both persons involved and their individual needs (13). This can be seen in **individualized consideration**, the third of the "5 Is" as it is all about people-orientation, where a leader knows team members as individuals, which enables them to get the best out of each person. To achieve individualised consideration, seeing people as complex human beings, with strengths and weaknesses, hinges on the leader **choosing to care** about people and taking the time to do so. No one size fits all leadership approach can apply when people are so different, and leaders have to acknowledge these differences. However, when willing to make the effort, the pay off, based on people feeling appreciated, is increased engagement and improved performance.

Showing Personal Appreciation

A leader must manage both the organization's needs and ensure all team members are involved, included, motivated and able to contribute to the overall team and organizational success. Though tasks can be defined to achieve these activities, a true leader must have an intrinsic career motive that includes people involvement, people management and people development. In other words, to actually like people, not simply see a team as means to progress their career. Those with high task achievement motives may seek to grow or improve operations, yet risk putting too much pressure on others (79). Focus on team members requires humility, high emotional intelligence and an ability to share praise and **appreciation**.

According to Steven Covey, author of "The 7 Habits of Highly Effective People", "next to survival, the greatest need of a human being is… to be understood, affirmed, validated and appreciated" (151).

Research has also shown that employees are most satisfied and motivated through recognition of performance and achievement. Herzberg includes recognition as a motivator (144) and in McClelland's understanding of needs, the need for achievement, a part of all of us, is associated with desire for feedback on progress and achievement (23).

However, formal recognition can sometimes be perceived as predictable, routine and impersonal (152). What works better is personalised encouragement and recognition expressed from the heart. Feeling genuinely appreciated lifts people up, makes people feel safe, which frees them up to do their best work. When personal value feels at risk, worry becomes preoccupying, which drains and diverts energy from creating value (153). Feeling valued also helps avoid conflict, which according to Paul McGee, may have many reasons such as not being listened to, being overlooked, not consulted, yet the core impact is the same – people not feeling important. "Treating someone in a way that is unique to them is a powerful way to make that person feel important" and appreciated (87).

Appreciation can also impact the bottom line! Multiple studies have linked the engagement resulting from appreciation, with reduced turnover, lower absenteeism and increased productivity, all of which improve profitability. This includes published data from Glassdoor, Forbes, Bersin Associates and BCG:

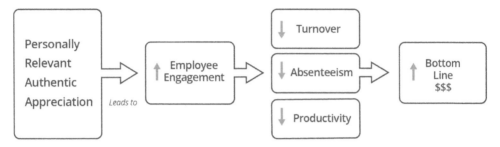

Figure 49: How Appreciation Impacts the Bottom Line

So, "thank you" really are two very powerful words and as rewards, certainly inexpensive. Studies into appreciation and the use of "thank you" does show dramatic impact. Researchers at University of Pennsylvania divided university fund-raisers into two groups to collect donations. The group told by the director that she was grateful for their efforts made 50% more fund-raising calls than those in the other group (154), concluding that people feel motivated to work harder when they hear thank you.

In other work to explain why gratitude motivates, Kouzes & Posner summarized many examples and reported that "personal congratulations rank at the top of motivators by employees" (152). So, spreading thanks can make a difference, however, on the flip side, "gratitude is an attainment associated with emotional maturity" so may not motivate all employees all the time (154).

Acting with Empathy and Engaging in Genuine Dialogue

Engaging employees as individuals also requires a leader to connect with people on a deeper level. This comes from high emotional intelligence, especially high inter-personal skills, also known as social intelligence, and includes understanding other people, what motivates others, how they work and how to work cooperatively with them (75, 76). It also means understanding how others feel and choosing to care about this to behave more appropriately, allowing the management of relationships more effectively.

In chapter 5 we introduced emotional intelligence and focused on the "self" parts. To connect with others, it is the elements of empathy and social skills that count:

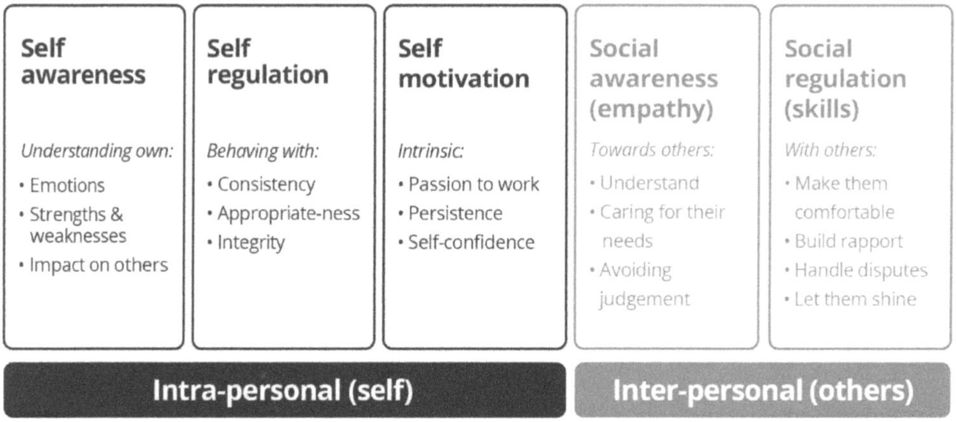

Self awareness	**Self regulation**	**Self motivation**	**Social awareness (empathy)**	**Social regulation (skills)**
Understanding own:	*Behaving with:*	*Intrinsic:*	*Towards others:*	*With others:*
• Emotions	• Consistency	• Passion to work	• Understand	• Make them comfortable
• Strengths & weaknesses	• Appropriate-ness	• Persistence	• Caring for their needs	• Build rapport
• Impact on others	• Integrity	• Self-confidence	• Avoiding judgement	• Handle disputes
				• Let them shine

Intra-personal (self)	**Inter-personal (others)**

Figure 50: The Elements of Emotional Intelligence

> *'I believe empathy is the most essential quality of civilisation'*
>
> ROGER EBERT (155)

Empathy is the ability to understand the emotional makeup of other people – to identify with and understand the wants, needs and viewpoints of those in a team. It is essential to create trust between people.

Leaders with high empathy can:

* Recognise the feelings of others even when those feelings may not be obvious
* Listen well – listening to understand, not to interrupt
* Relate well to others – and respond to others concerns
* Be available when others need them
* Avoid stereotyping and judging too quickly
* Manage relationships well

There are 3 parts of empathy (156):

Cognitive empathy is knowing that you need to treat people individually to communicate in a way that others understand, putting it in their terms.

Emotional empathy is the ability to sense or feel what the other person is feeling, so putting yourself in their shoes.

Empathic concern is the deepest level meaning thinking, feeling and actually caring about the other person, so genuinely saying "I understand" or "I care".

Emotional intelligence guru Daniel Goleman describes this last level meaning "I know how you feel, I know what you need, I'm predisposed to help you if I can". He calls this "the caring system of the brain" and Goleman's view is that humanity needs compassion in order to survive (156).

In his studies however, he has found correlation between willingness to display empathy and compassion, with time constraints. This may go some way to explain why leaders struggle as they are too focused on operational tasks. In a Hays survey in 2014, "79% of managers said they had too little time for leadership tasks, yet only 9% said they had too little time for managerial tasks" (157).

To appreciate another person, it is essential to get to know them. This means going beyond the fact discussions and technical talk about tasks. It requires time commitment and a desire to engage in genuine dialogue. It works in the context of building trust and requires solid communication skills in asking questions and listening. **Genuine dialogue** has the intention is to establish a mutual relationship. It occurs when participants have the other in mind, it is about exploring ideas together and it uses all modes of communication – questioning, appreciating, recommending, informing and sharing (86).

In order to get the best of out of each person, a leader has to explore strengths, weaknesses, development areas, career aspirations and motivators. An effective way to do so is to simply ask…. We all have a desire to improve our lives and most will tell what works for them! But getting to know someone else involves curiosity. When was the last time you really asked someone what makes them happy? Understanding motives can also come from asking questions such as:

* What brings you most satisfaction?
* Describe a time when you felt particularly motivated at work?
* In order for you to feel valued and appreciated by someone, what would they need to do to demonstrate that?
* Is there one thing I could do to support you that I am not currently doing?

Choosing to be a leader must be driven by intrinsic care of other people. It is the leader's responsibility to connect with people, learn what motivates them, use this to challenge them and show people appreciation for who they are and what they contribute, thereby gaining commitment and performance. Paul McGee, author of many books on influence also believes that leveraging all emotional intelligence skills can enable a leader to make people feel "SPECIAL" (87) by serving, personalising, encouraging, showing courtesy, interest and appreciation, and finally really listening to the other person to show care:

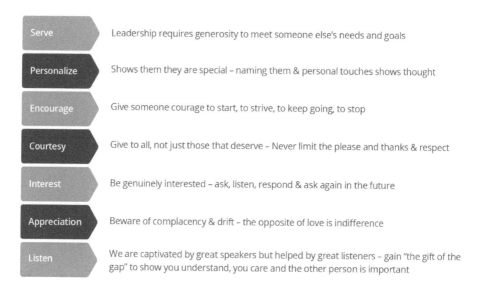

Figure 51: **How to Make People Feel SPECIAL (87)**

Acting as a Coach

Within the framework of transformational leadership, being in the coaching role is **empowering others to succeed**, not telling people what to do, but listening and supporting them in finding their own solution. The challenge is that if time is the predominant criterion, doing the job yourself or telling someone exactly what to do will be the fastest way. However, supporting individual development and creating new learning opportunities pays off in the long run as team members become more knowledgeable, self-directed and self-sufficient.

Coaching is a process that aims to improve performance with the coach as a facilitator of learning. As Confucius said, "Tell me, and I will forget. Show me, and I will remember. Involve me, and I will understand." This point and the power of coaching can be seen with data on recall. In experiments at IBM and UK Post Office and referenced by coaching expert Sir John Whitmore (158), people were divided in 3 groups and taught a simple task by one of the 3 approaches. Telling alone has limited recall on how to do the task after 3 months (only 10% recall), whereas coaching, when people receive explanation, demonstration and hands on practice, increases recall to 65%.

Coaching also has benefits for the individual and the organization. For individuals, they are more motivated as they feel nurtured, and they gain new perspectives and skills for job enhancement and career development. Using other internal coaches, coachees can also broaden organizational exposure and networks. For the organization itself, when well implemented, coaching is a powerful tool in employee development and succession planning as employees are prepared for new roles. The action of internal development and progression also engages, builds stronger teams and creates a nimble workforce.

The power of coaching is also linked to mind set. It requires ability and willingness of the coachee to grow and change. Stanford professor Carol Dweck (59) called this a **growth mind set**, when people see their abilities as learned traits which can be developed. Such people are open to challenges and new experiences and see failure as a chance to learn. On the other hand, people with a **fixed mind set** see intelligence and personality as static features. For them, success is about proving talent or smartness and failure means that you just don't have what it takes. Such people tend to avoid new situations and take constructive feedback personally. People with a fixed mind set are much less receptive to coaching than those with a growth mind set.

The aim of coaching is to increase a skill or competency for a job or task, through building on existing knowledge and continuing to expand experiences. The outcome should be enhanced performance in that defined area and the responsibility for performance outcomes lies with the coachee. However, to move from a current performance level to enhanced performance, requires several steps with differing actions from coach and coachee:

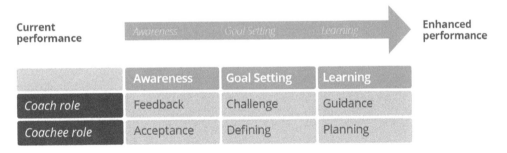

Figure 52: The Roles of Coach and Coachee

Awareness of the development area can occur from self-reflection or a coach may give feedback. The coachee must agree there is a gap though and have a desire for development. Setting goals is about identifying what the coachee actually wants to achieve. The direction and target can be challenged by the coach, yet the goal must be defined by coachee to be inspiring, challenging, to push them to grow. Creating and executing a learning plan can also have elements guided by the coach, yet ownership lies with the coachee to plan how to develop, what other tools they may need alongside coaching, and when it will all happen.

The Essence of Good Coaching

Both coach and coachee must understand that **responsibility** on the part of the coachee is the essence of good coaching. As leader and coach, it is knowing that your role is unlocking the other person's potential to maximise performance on their own. It is helping the other to learn rather than teaching them. It is raising awareness of the development need and opportunity for the coachee. As such, the coachee must also be open to the learning experience and their responsibility for their performance. Good coaches believe that the individual always has the answer to their own problems but understands that they may need help to find the answer. Qualities to unlock another's potential include patience, interest, attentiveness, good perspective and ability to listen.

Coaching uses **skills** including:

* Open questioning to cause others to think for themselves
* Active listening, to understand what other is truly saying
* Focus on detail, forcing an in-depth look at issues and options, probing for more factors that may be important
* Blind spots are things unknown to the coachee yet known to others and can include behaviours or skills. A coach can seek to build awareness in such areas to begin rectification of a flaw or enhancement of a strength
* Finally, reflecting back and summarising key points ensures correct understanding between both parties

To be effective, coaching requires agreed rules and structures. This can include behavioural expectations and agendas for regular meetings. Many coaches use the **GROW model**, developed by Whitmore (158), as a guideline to prepare and to conduct sessions. This model structures the conversation into four steps, is simple to use and comprehensive:

Goals: uncovering what the person is trying to achieve, their thinking on scale, scope and specificity on the current challenge. Setting short- and long-term goals.

Reality: exploring the situation – what is happening inside and around the challenge, in terms of where they are, the history, the other players, context, processes, constraints etc. What are others thinking and doing?

Options: what different courses of action does the person have in mind? Could this be expanded or focused? Can more outside the box thinking and alternatives help?

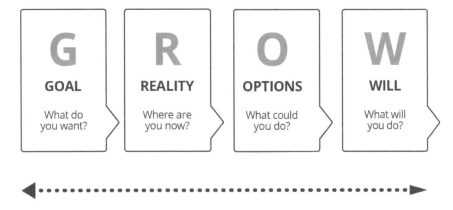

Figure 53: Representation of the GROW Model for Coaching (158)

Willingness: what psychological and material resources are required to move forward on the issue? How ready and committed is the person to do what it takes and follow through? Then plan what, when, who…

Coaching only works when it is in a high trust relationship and that trust is maintained, for example, through confidentiality (160). It must be a structured process and yet has boundaries, for example topics that will not be covered. Clear expectations of both parties must be known, and it is time defined based on achieving the goal or when it has outgrown its usefulness. As a leader coaching an employee, the ability and willingness of the employee must also be considered. Coaching must be aligned with individual profile and development goals. Employees always need ability, but more specifically, willingness for a task, role, project, development etc. (161). This latter point can also be considered alongside the concept of **situational leadership**. This model by Hersey and Blanchard (162, 163) is a useful tool for assigning new tasks and developing employees based on building experience and delegating to employees. Delegation however is more than task assignment as it is also giving responsibility for decisions and actions, and as such full delegation should occur only when employees are capable and skilled. Until that point, the leader needs to balance direction and freedom to operate with the individual's ability to perform the new task. Coaching is a phase within such a learning approach and this model by Hersey & Blanchard shows the changes required in the leaders' behaviour as the individual gains new skills to complete a task. It is based on the experience and maturity of the individual and as such, the leader needs to know the employee well.

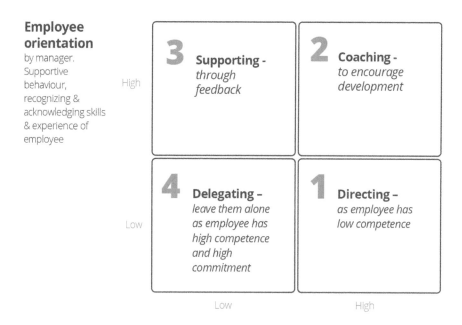

Figure 54: Representation of Situational Leadership Applied to Coaching

Following the model, the flow can be seen from assigning a new task:

Directing [1]: The employee may demonstrate low competence towards the new task, and therefore more directing is needed focused on that actual task.

Coaching [2]: Over time, less direction is required on the task and the shift is towards encouraging development through coaching.

Supporting [3]: Even less involvement is required, little instruction on the task and only support through feedback is needed as the employee becomes more skilled.

Delegating [4]: Finally, the individual can be left alone, with full delegation of the task, as they are fully competent and able to succeed.

In summary, the coaching mind set requires a leader to step back and allow others to find their way. Challenging under time pressure yet rewarding in terms of getting the most out of individuals for greater success and very different from a directive management approach. Coaching is a powerful tool to prepare and empower others to succeed. As a leader it means supporting employees in finding their own solutions and through this, team members become more knowledgeable, self-directed and self-sufficient! The contrasting views can be seen here:

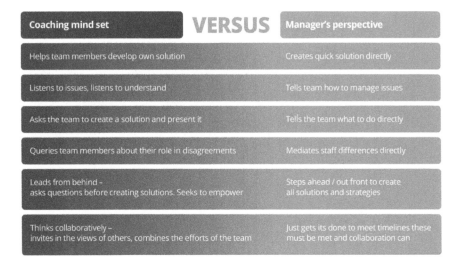

Coaching mind set	VERSUS	Manager's perspective
Helps team members develop own solution		Creates quick solution directly
Listens to issues, listens to understand		Tells team how to manage issues
Asks the team to create a solution and present it		Tells the team what to do directly
Queries team members about their role in disagreements		Mediates staff differences directly
Leads from behind – asks questions before creating solutions. Seeks to empower		Steps ahead / out front to create all solutions and strategies
Thinks collaboratively – invites in the views of others, combines the efforts of the team		Just gets its done to meet timelines these must be met and collaboration can

Figure 55: The Coaching Mind Set

We have considered the leader's role in coaching, yet other people can be valuable for supporting and challenging thinking and enhancing performance in other ways. Whereas a manager may focus on a current or operational task related to a coachee's job, a senior manager in a more strategic role could focus development on competencies related to long term planning or strategic direction. They may also facilitate the connections between people and improve communication lines. Peer coaching is a procedure of learning which can reflect or accompany actual work in practice and aims at the further development of practical skills using the experiences and competencies of team members to solve problems for example.

The Adage of Mentorship

Mentoring is not the same as coaching. Though both are learning methodologies (164), coaching requires stepping back and allow others to find their way and facilitating learning. Coaching is focused on a current skill or competency gap related to current job or tasks or near job. Mentoring on the other hand is future oriented, considering a person's path forward and as such can look at broader competency expansion such as leadership skills. A mentor can be a colleague, but one who has an emotional investment, can share personal experiences and offer advice on how they would approach a situation. As such they can be inspiring as a role model. They can also open doors, give access to new networks. It is about growth. However, like coaching, mentorship also works hand in hand with other learning actions and as part of a well-conceived and goal-oriented personal development plan.

Though mentorship goes back to ancient Greek times, in current understanding, the mentor´s function is to allow the mentee to benefit from their experiences and to accompany the individual career development of the mentee (165). The focus lies on generating new or broader perspectives, developing strategic approaches, implementing new behaviours and gaining access to networks. Within an organization, mentorship and championing of talented individuals increases exposure to senior leaders, shapes development and prepares people better for new roles.

Mentoring is a proven and powerful tool for **career development** (166). A direct line manager however may not always be best placed to mentor team members, but instead coach on current role-specific gaps. More senior leaders, even those outside the organization, are better placed to mentor talents and great leaders not only give of themselves generously to mentor others, they often seek out those with potential whom they can support or sponsor for future growth.

Recognizing Individual Strengths and Developing Accordingly

Individualized consideration extends beyond an openness to coaching people, to also include a structured approach to recognizing individuals' strengths and creating effective development plans. This can also be described by the leadership competency **employee development**, defined as a line manager developing team members' skills by planning effective actions related to current and future tasks and considering individual motivations and interests. This is challenging in terms of the time requirement to carefully listen to individual needs and implement effective plans. It is also especially challenging as many wrongly believe it is the role of HR. Not only is it the responsibility of a leader to develop their team members and enable them to grow as individuals, but leaders are the only ones close enough to do this. Through regular dialogue with each employee, leaders gain insights and can therefore define which development action is best suited for the organizational and individual needs. Yes, it is essential that any leader understands the Talent Strategy or HR strategy of their organization, which includes key elements for bringing people into an organization and how they are managed once on board, yet the overall responsibility for people, lies with the leader.

'Talent is developed at work, by individual managers who take on the greatest responsibility of doing so'

ALISTAIR DRYBURGH (167)

An HR framework should include recruitment, competencies defining desired behaviours that can be hired for and developed, development programs for strategically relevant competencies, career paths linked to organizational structure, systematic and structured succession planning for filling key positions, compensation and benefits goals and policies, and retention plans for high potentials and top talents. Such a framework is established to support a performance culture, deliver company goals and overall business success (168).

The Leader's Role in Employee Development

Figure 56: The Employee Development Process

A leader must engage with employees regularly and take time to listen carefully to their individual needs (45) and nurture their uniqueness. It is also the leader's responsibility to provide appropriate work challenges, which can be defined in job descriptions and goals. Furthermore, a leader needs awareness of employee's strengths and development areas based on performance in their current role and future organizational needs. It is then a partnership between leader and employee to prepare realistic development plans and ensure support is appropriate for employees to reach their personal goals, as well as business goals. This can be provision of tools or training for a task. Lastly, leaders must provide honest and constructive feedback regarding performance and behaviour.

In this context, individualization counts. If a leader is unaware of the skill level and needs of each team member, they will be unable to bring out the best in each one. They may also inadvertently create anxiety. Using the **Flow Model**, first introduced by psychologist Mihaly Csíkszentmihályi in 1990 (169), it suggests emotional states people are likely to experience when trying to complete a task, depending on the perceived difficulty of the challenge, and their perceptions of skill levels:

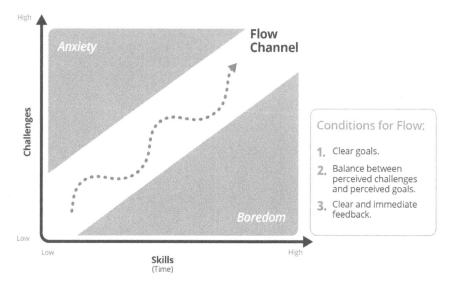

Figure 57: Representation of the Flow Model for Performance Effectiveness (169)

If the task isn't challenging and doesn't require a lot of skill, people are likely to feel apathy towards it. But facing a challenging task without the required skills could easily result in worry and anxiety. To perform at best, people need a challenge that is significant and interesting, and well-developed skills, so they are confident to meet the challenge. In this position people can experience "flow" and are totally involved and engaged in the activity. Csíkszentmihályi also identified three things that must be present to enter a state of flow: Goals add motivation and structure to what people do; there must be a good balance between perceived skill and perceived challenge of the task; people must have clear, immediate feedback, so they can make changes and improve performance. This can be feedback from other people, or the awareness that they are making progress with the task.

Assessment of Performance

The assessment and development of employees is also part of an overall process called **performance management** (170). Many companies run formal Performance Management Processes as a way to link individual goals to business objectives and standardise the assessment. This generally includes mandatory appraisal meetings in which leaders and employees discuss and document performance over the last year and consider future goals and development actions. Effective performance management can achieve higher employee engagement and reduced turnover.

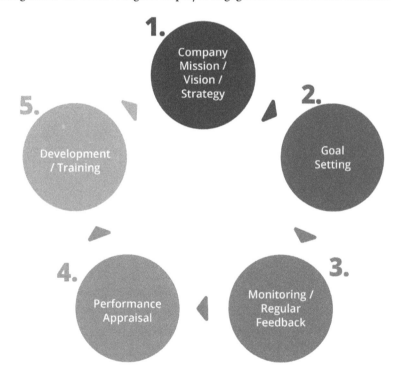

Figure 58: The Performance Management Process

Reviewing the strengths, weaknesses or development areas, must be objective and avoid bias by the assessor. It should therefore consider pre-defined and transparent criteria including results of achievement of SMART goals set for the period and expected skill and knowledge required for a person's current role and tasks, as defined in their job profile. Many companies also assess the demonstration of competencies, the success behaviours desired in that company and the transferable abilities that facilitate agility and flexibility on the part of the organization, such as effective communication, decision making and customer orientation. Overall impression of commitment and attitude are often reviewed as this relates to "how we do things round here" or more formal company values. From this, the leader's responsibility is to reward completion or over achievement of goals and manage under-achievement when required in a constructive manner. Any gaps in skills or knowledge for the current role or tasks can also be rectified with development opportunities or targeted training.

Strength-Based Development

In dialogue with employees, leaders will uncover areas where individuals over-achieve versus expectations or under achieve. Human nature has a tendency to focus on what is lacking and short-term solutions may involve shoring up these deficits. However, an alternative is to understand the differences and position people so they use more of who they are and what their strengths are, in other words, their talents (171, 172). Measurement of talent or strengths provides a framework around positive psychological potential. When people become aware of their talents, through measurement and feedback, they have a strong position from which to develop. They can then begin to integrate their awareness of their talents with knowledge and skills to develop strengths even further (171). Strength-based development helps employees identify, cultivate and use their strengths at work. It enables success and enhances employee well-being (173). And as Alex Linley defined strength-based development, "it is authentic and energizing to the user, and enables optimal functioning, development and performance" (172).

Employee development should be framed in the context of company vision, strategy and goals, yet is delivered individually to motivate, retain, nurture and grow. Not only should employee development look to maximise performance in current roles, it should also look to develop employees with the potential to move into new roles, more senior roles or take on more significant responsibility. It must also consider the aspirations and ambitions of the employee as it is their career.

Career management is the process that involves career exploration, development of career goals, and use of career strategies to obtain career goals. This can be individually driven and augmented with leadership support. Leaders play a critical role in employee careers and data from McKinsey's Women in the Workplace Survey 2017 (174) showed that leaders are especially central to women's success as the leaders' actions can have a big impact on aspiration and progression.

For the individual, career planning is the process of making and implementing informed decisions, starting from understanding strengths to leverage (skills and competencies), experiences gained, personal values and career goals. Having a development plan to close any gaps in skills, competencies or experience, can be created in conjunction between leader and employee for full business and personal alignment.

Development plans for employees should also following the **70/20/10 Learning Concept** (61) introduced in chapter 3, with string focus on on-the-job development. This results in high performance quicker and builds new skills for career progression. Combined with insightful feedback, powerful plans can be implemented for effective learning and development, and individually tailored.

Where Feedback Fits

Feedback in itself is a very powerful development tool and how it fits with coaching is also important to note. So, what sorts of feedback are there (175)?

3 types of feedback

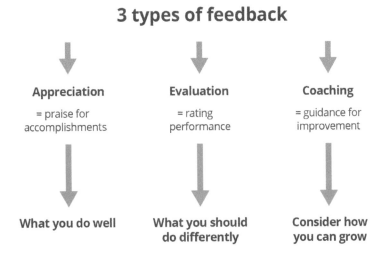

Appreciation	Evaluation	Coaching
= praise for accomplishments	= rating performance	= guidance for improvement
What you do well	What you should do differently	Consider how you can grow

Figure 59: Summary of Three Types of Feedback

Firstly, appreciation is a form of recognition and motivation and should be given for who someone is and what they do well. It should not be combined with an improving or learning message.

Secondly, evaluation relates to performance and is part of the assessment and performance review managers undertake during annual appraisals for example.

The third type of feedback is when coaching to improve performance.

To give insightful feedback (176, 177) that is more likely to be accepted, the message must be specific and concrete, with examples. It must be based upon personal observations, not interpretations or valuation. It should be useful for the receiver, seemingly valuable for their development. With a manager or leader as feedback giver, it is credible, especially within a trusting relationship. A lead is also well placed to share feedback with support and interest in the others' development. Yet to be open to receive, the employee needs self-confidence for acceptance. Feedback must however be presented as a gift and if it is an unwelcome gift, the giver must also accept this.

The Final Link to Workforce Planning

Transformational leaders treat people as individuals, however in the context of current and future business success, leaders also need to consider their team portfolio and manage the performance and development of the entire team. This also highlights why assessment requires structure, criteria and objectivity – whenever a leader undertakes employee assessments, they must be responsible for that assessment, follow through on actions and be cognitive of the consequences for individuals and teams.

Leaders have to make decisions on hiring, promotions, new assignments and longer-term workforce planning, such as succession planning. In order to make good decisions, leaders can use tools such as a 9-box grid for people management (178). Plotting a team on such a grid by measurement of performance in their current role and assessment of future potential can give indications of actions for individuals as well as priorities for development investments.

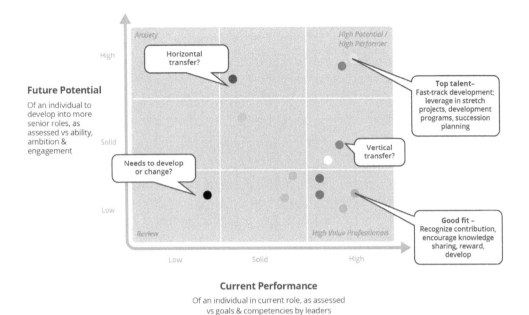

Figure 60: Representation of a Nine-Box Grid for Talent Mapping

Though many leaders many be familiar with the measurement of current performance, this looks backwards at historic results and does not always indicate future success. Considering future potential is about looking forward and should include ability and capacity for growth and ability to perform effectively in other roles. Such **future-directed assessment** can be made in Development Centres or by leaders and criteria should include: Ability (demonstration of key Competencies); Ambition; Engagement with the organization. Once again it allows leaders to see employees as individuals, value individuals and also develop those with the desire to take on more responsibility, thus preparing an organization of the future.

In summary, the third I of the **extended Transformational Leadership model**, "individualized consideration" is linked to strong people orientation and considers *how* to show care to others respect for individuals, and enable others to develop and grow. To bring this concept further to life, here are examples of actions from highly successful global leaders.

What Individualized Consideration Looks Like in Practice

'Choosing to care is across the board – it is not linked to position or title – it is being friendly and open to everyone and treating all equally, even if you don't know them'. *Peer M. Schatz.*

"It's imperative leaders genuinely and actively listen and get to know their employees – what goes on personally, as well as at work. It's about overall well-being – financial, physical and mental. This isn't about simply ticking the one-to-one box to keep HR quiet for monthly meetings and appraisals, this is about caring for and knowing your team!" *Alison Staley, HR Consultant and Chartered Fellow of Chartered Institute of Personnel and Development.*

"It is easy to coach and support those who ask. It is also important to consider the quieter team members who work hard and perform well day in and day out yet are modest with their achievements or needs. Take time to recognize and support them too!" *Peer M. Schatz.*

"When managing teams, you often have a mix of people who are genuinely motivated and driven and others that may need more nudging now and then to perform at a higher level. For those who are highly motivated, it is just as important to make sure they do to not overload themselves as it is to manage the performance of those who are not so driven. This is the same balance needed such as focusing on positive elements when providing feedback and building in some of the things that need improvement. People are much more motivated to work on their development areas if they feel they also get acknowledgement for all the positive things they do." *Thomas Schweins, Senior Vice President, QIAGEN.*

"What I have learnt is that if you are having a conversation with someone you have to be fully present, focused entirely on them and not distracted or diverted by anything else". *Peer M. Schatz.*

"It is better to trust more than not at all. Yes, some people will let you down, but it should never stop you giving everyone a chance". *Peer M. Schatz.*

Key Learning Points

- Individualized consideration means treating all employees with respect and valuing their contributions
- Managing people requires completion of tasks related to performance management and employee development
- Leading people hinges on choosing to care about people, even showing compassion in the workplace
- Appreciation is the foundation of care, when genuine and personalized, and it can impact the bottom line
- Empathy is born out of high emotional intelligence and as such must be well developed in leaders; it is also more than cognitive understanding; it must be demonstrated, such as through genuine dialogue
- Coaching is focused on a current skill or competency gap related to current job or tasks or near job
- Coaching is an ideal learning tool for leaders to utilize within teams. Not only does it have impact on individual performance and team agility, it also increases confidence, knowledge and self-sufficiency
- Coaching is also appropriate alongside assignment of new and challenging tasks
- Mentoring is future oriented, considering a person's path forward and as such can look at broader competency expansion such as leadership skills for overall career development
- Individual development is best focused around strengths and talents
- All individuals should have a personal development plan and receive constructive feedback from their manager on performance, behaviours and overall contribution
- Team development should also fit organization goals and future plans

Personal Reflection Points

Question 1: How well do you know the people in your team?

How often do you have growth and development discussions with individuals?

Do you use and advocate coaching as a learning methodology?

Does each member of your team have a personal development plan?

How would your team rate your empathetic dialogue?

Question 2: How do you recognize the contributions of others? Give examples.

What else could you do?

Chapter 10
Empowering People to Think

Key Knowledge...

- The 4th I, intellectual stimulation, describes how to challenge the status quo and establish an overall environment for innovation, allowing all to contribute to decision making, problem solving and success

Key Actions...

- Establish working ways that are flexible and agile, providing freedom to innovate
- Create an environment for innovation: demonstrating a mind set for curiosity and creative thinking and establishing processes for collaborative teamwork
- Actively leverage diversity

Impacts...

- Empowering people to think and work more collaboratively transforms the way they develop products, processes and strategies
- Encouraging participation and collaboration by removing barriers and control unlocks the potential of people to think freely and to come up with new ideas
- Leveraging the diverse experiences and ideas from all team members brings new perspectives, more creativity, better decision making and overall enhanced team performance

Intellectual stimulation focuses on the leader's role in providing the freedom to think differently. Business competitiveness really does mean being better than the competitor companies over a sustainable period of time. Such improvements and innovations only come from challenging the status quo, breaking away from old ways and embracing new ideas. Yes, this can be risky but the payoff great. It is why such values are currently at the top of many company agendas.

'The task of a leader is to get people from where
they are to a place they have not been'

HENRY KISSINGER (179)

Establishing Flexibility and Agility in Teams

Leading by fostering intellectual stimulation signifies that leaders encourage their employees to develop creative ideas and actively challenge them to question the status-quo. In the words of Bass and Riggio "the leader gets others to look at problems from many different angles" (67). Employees are encouraged and supported in looking at problems in new ways and questioning established convictions, patterns and ideas. This gets them directly involved in the solution-finding process.

With new and innovative approaches, mistakes are inevitable. But in the context of developing creative ideas and going new ways, the leader does not criticize, but tolerates these mistakes. Moreover, the leader plays the role of a stimulating and steering problem-solver. This creates an intelligent handling of problems and an open environment where employees can develop their own ideas.

One such approach that embraces empowered thinking with delivery of results is **agile** (180). Agility became the buzz word of modern business to speed up organizations' ability to change. Agile working methods produce transparency and flexibility and stimulate thinking processes. Agile values were born out of a need for faster and better-quality software development in the 1990s, yet application for Agile has extended to many industries due to its emphasis on lean manufacturing, collaboration, communication and quick development with smaller feature changes. There are now several agile project management tools, such as Scrum (181) and Kanban. The management methods of the these may vary however the values and principles of each tool are consistent.

Agile working values are: Commitment, Focus, Courage, Respect, as well as Openness.

Principles of agile working methods are: Transparency; empowered, self-organized teams; delivery of product early, with regular update; inspecting and adapt when it doesn't work.

The overall purpose is not only facilitating individuals to engage and think differently, the whole organization is more flexible to deal with change quickly, without massive disruption. As the business world of today is shaped by the need to adapt to constant change, both organizations and leaders require more agility to make rapid changes, rearrange rather than restructure, and respond with actions that are focused, fast and flexible.

Dr Nick Horney, agile leadership expert, developed a list of agility skills for leaders to achieve this (26) and grouped into abilities to:

- Anticipate Change – by understanding and tracking forces of change that influence success
- Generate Confidence – by connecting, aligning and engaging all stakeholders
- Initiate Action – establishing an execution culture with a sense of urgency, capacity for decision making and collaboration.
- Liberate Thinking – establishing permission and expectations for innovation from all levels, with a customer focus.
- Evaluate Results – providing timely and accurate feedback on key success measures

When compared to many of the behavioural anchors of extended transformational leadership, the overlap is significant, indicative of transformational leadership's proven success in change scenarios. In the context of intellectual stimulation and empowering others to think, once again creating the environmental framework and inviting participation augments concepts to "liberate thinking" as Horney puts it.

Another methodology for achieving more flexibility or agility is the **design thinking** approach as "thinking like a designer can transform the way you develop products, services, processes – and even strategy". Design thinking was developed at Stanford University and can be described as a human-centered, collaborative, optimistic and experimental approach (182). It again aims to identify urgent problems and requires empathy and in-depth understanding of the needs and wishes of people, such as customers. It is also based on an optimistic belief that change can be created, and that no matter how challenging the constraints of given problems are, at least one possible solution is better than the existing option. It is also experimental where mistakes are allowed since failure creates new ideas. Finally, design thinking is a team based, cross disciplinary process which supports different points of view and enhances creativity through diversity.

As a method, design thinking embraces five steps:
Step 1: Empathize: Analyze problems of the target group
Step 2: Define: Focus on the one problem you wish to solve
Step 3: Ideate: Thinking differently, using creative methods, like brainstorming and mind mapping
Step 4: Prototype: The chance for failure. Experiment with ideas to find out if they really solve the problem
Step 5: Test: Decide on one way to go and test it on the target group.

Empowering people to think and work more collaboratively and transparently can transform the way they develop products, processes and even strategies. With today's need for people and organizations to be flexible to adapt to constant change and remain competitive, liberating thinking can only help!

Creating an Environment for Innovation

Though many companies today strive for innovation, simply telling people to be creative is not enough. It is important that organizational culture and structure do not work against this. Fostering intellectual stimulation or stimulating employees to be creative and innovative requires leaders to manage the environment and actively remove any barriers to free thinking. Through consideration of mind set, competencies and structure, leaders can create a more open climate for innovation. The following actions are required:

Group Think Has to Stop: Firstly, for a more productive and open mind set and a creative and critical thinking atmosphere, groupthink has to stop. Groupthink is an exaggerated striving for harmony and agreement, especially in very homogeneous groups (183). Stress, bad communication or missing neutrality of the leader are other important aspects and overall, this endangers realistic assessments and decision-making.

Groupthink can be recognized when a group overestimates itself, decisions are not being questioned and not all relevant information is gathered – especially when the information is not positive. A further symptom is the missing reflection of different options and the missing evaluation and review of the final solution (183).

Groupthink is not a given for every team, but even in teams that usually work together very well, groupthink can happen, especially in stress situations. These can be caused by external factors such as a new customer demand in a limited timeframe or internal issues when people refuse to engage in discussion. As Harley Lovegrove notes, "agreeing with someone is much less hassle than rejecting their idea head on" (184). However, demonstrating intellectual curiosity means to keep seeking for understanding, new truths and new ideas.

All Voices Have to be Heard: To involve all people in finding new and better ways leaders need to ensure all voices are heard, not just the loudest ones. For a leader, this must be an active process to seek out different views, ask for contributions from everyone and give time for thinking. Conventions and cross-functional boundaries also need to be ignored to gather inputs from experts, regardless of rank. Especially in a group setting, a leader must ask for inputs, not simply giving their opinion. They must specifically direct questions at quieter team members to avoid loss of all perspectives and they must challenge given statements and norms to ensure new ideas surface. To overcome group anxieties, email or separate one-to-one sessions can be employed encourage participation when necessary. See the easyJet example for more ideas.

Failure Has to be Allowed: As Sochiro Honda, the founder of Honda, once said: "Success is 99% failure." Though failure itself does not lead directly to innovation, it is the way failure is dealt with that matters (185). A culture of failure means a culture of trust and constructive criticism, where errors are accepted and not punished. A destructive handling of failure, where mistakes are denied and covered up, leads to a demotivation of employees. But a positive culture of failure leads to motivation, learning and involvement. Believe it or not, there are organizations who have a corporate culture where failure is permitted and even desired. An example for such a company is Google.

The Google Example (186)

Fear of failure is more prevalent in large organizations than start-ups. In big companies, middle managers thrive on stability and predictability, yet entrepreneurs tend to be risk takers who are psychologically prepared to fail many times on their way to success. Google understood this friction from the beginning and in 2012 undertook even more efforts to improve their culture, by setting out to understand exactly what makes teams more innovative and effective (Project Aristotle):

Creating a culture of acceptance – accepting failure but also stupid ideas, silly mistakes, contradictory thoughts, and wasted money. Understanding that not every project has to be approved and there needs to be a rigorous filtering and selection process. And agreeing that the person behind any crazy idea should not be criticised.

Making teams more creative – Google experimented with teams and found that the answer to making teams more creative was in how the team members treated one another. Teams that encouraged everyone to participate scored much better. Also, teams with higher social sensitivity, performed better as a group. These two factors could raise a group's collective intelligence and productivity far above a group with more experienced and accomplished individuals.

Psychological safety – Groups whose members felt the most secure speaking their minds performed best. The more open and accepted people feel, the better they cooperate and think together as a single unit. Such teams openly debate, interrupt one another, and discuss every aspect of everything.

Finally, google carefully documents and distributes the learnings from any mistake – team members reflect on the learnings and a report is available for every team member and provides the team and future teams with a lasting resource that they can turn to whenever necessary. They call it their Post-mortem Philosophy.

This culture, where everyone can participate without fear of losing status or being criticised, has been one of their keys to successful innovation.

"For us, it's not about pointing fingers at any given person or team, but about using what we've learned to build resilience and prepare for future issues that may arise along the way. By discussing our failures in public and working together to investigate their root causes, everyone gets the opportunity to learn from each incident and to be involved with any next steps." (187)

New thinking: What is creativity and creative thinking? Creativity actually means the use of imagination or original ideas to create something; inventiveness. However, innovation is the taking of something that already exists and using it in a new way (184). Surely therefore innovation is a more achievable organizational goal? For innovation to flourish, it requires leaders to establish and maintain the environment to stimulate a more **creative-type thinking** though.

The frequently heard expression may be "**thinking outside the box**" again to create something radically different. So instead of thinking outside the box, innovation often involves thinking differently about the box (188). Often the solution is near, people only have to take a step back and look at things from a different angle.

The other difficulty is that in our imagination, when we think about problems or reaching goals, we form patterns. These patterns are self-imposed boundaries or barriers, that keep our thinking in a framework. We constrain our own thinking in this way (189).

This "box" in our head represents our **assumptions** and we all have assumptions about the way something is or the way something should be. So, thinking outside the box is another term for challenging our assumptions. In business, there are no standard assumptions, but Rigie and Harmeyer try to list you a few common ones in the organizational context (190):

"Things are always going this way"

"There is just no simple solution to this problem, it is just too complicated!"

"We do not have enough money to realize this project"

A transformational leader must question these assumptions and challenge employees to think outside the box in their head.

The easyJet Example (191)

In work begun at airline easyJet and in conjunction with Time to Think plc, a concept called The Thinking Environment was created. Underlying the concept is a recognition that to develop organizational effectiveness, people must be able to think for themselves – every day, at every meeting and in every interaction. What they discovered however is that this is not linked to IQ, education, experience or power. The key factor for clear thinking and greater creativity is the way people are treated by those they are with while they are thinking. From this work they also defined 10 key enablers most effective to improve thinking:

Attention Listening with palpable respect and without interruption

Equality Giving equal turns to think and speak

Ease Offering freedom from internal urgency

Incisive Questions Finding and removing untrue assumptions that distort thinking

Information Supplying the facts and dismantling denial

Diversity Ensuring divergent thinking and diverse group identities

Encouragement Giving courage for independent thinking by removing internal competition

Feelings Allowing sufficient emotional release to restore thinking

Appreciation Practising a 5:1 ratio of appreciation to criticism

Place Creating a physical environment that says to people: "You matter".

The results of such an approach at easyJet included:

- Improved cooperation between pilots and managers which in turn led to a review of pilots' terms and conditions, which had been causing retention problems.
- A voluntary development program established from the thinking environment was oversubscribed nearly 3 times.
- Six years after set up, the culture committee continues to influence internal communication at easyJet and contribute to high levels of performance in the face of the relentless challenges facing the airline industry.

Empowering others to think, be flexible and be innovative is not all about a flash of inspiration. Moreover, creative ideas are the result of the right environment, including systematic processes (192). This can be achieved in what is described as an entrepreneurial climate where the purpose is exploration and innovation, responding to and exploiting change. Structure, rewards and culture emphasise strategic orientation and pursuit of opportunities, rather than being preoccupied with control. When there is a lack of innovation, it is often not because people are not creative, it is because people are hampered to be creative by hierarchies and control (192).

An innovative, entrepreneurial climate can deliver significant performance advantage and added value when delivering growth strategies such as in dynamic environments and exploring new markets. This is based on the flexibility, openness to ideas and speed of change that may be achieved. The "can do" attitude that such cultures exhibit can also impact positively on efficiency and productivity in times of pressure. The team spirit and support in such organizations leads to strong cross-functional interactions and cooperation (193).

Summary of a Climate for Innovation

Figure 61: **Summary of an Effective Climate for Innovation**

Finally let's look at some new working examples and the future of innovation as this topic will only continue in the global and digital world of increased connectedness.

Firstly, **co-innovation**, has been formally introduced in the last few years as a structured process that leads firms to collaborate with their customers, partners, and other stakeholders, because businesses came to understand that innovation cannot take place in a vacuum and requires different points of view, diverse skill sets and even more collaboration (194). Benefits have included: new commercial opportunities, increased chances of creating more new products and services that are successful, reduced overall cost of developing new products or services so improving a business's financial performance. It can also drive positive social impact. Examples of companies that are leveraging co-innovation: Tata Motors for its Nano car development and SAP and BMW utilize co-innovation lab concepts: global networks facilitating project-based development between the company, suppliers and customers.

Secondly, **innovation hubs** are often centrally funded bodies to enable national or cross-border collaboration, leveraging the expertise of partners for defined goals. These ecosystems of partners' facilities, factories, and classrooms for joint projects include the European Institute of Innovation & Technology networks. For example, the EIT Climate Innovation Hub in Germany focuses on sustainable city systems, e-mobility, solar energy, water and zero-carbon production. The EIT Digital Innovation Hub in Italy focuses on leveraging digital technologies to help improve quality of life. These are ongoing examples of connecting outside an organization for growth and innovation (195).

Leveraging the Power of Diversity

Stimulating employees to be creative means all possible perspectives, alternative solutions and options must be considered in planning and problem solving and decision making. The challenges to this include groupthink, the exaggerated desire for agreement and homogeneous teams. Homogeneous teams may be easy to manage and communication simple yet can result in no new ideas coming to the table and focus only on what is already known. The best way to solve this is by having heterogeneous or diverse teams. Why?

1. A diverse workforce allows the company to serve a diverse customer base better.
2. Diverse groups have different viewpoints, ideas, and market insights, which lead to superior performance.

'We need diversity of thought in the world
to face the new challenges'

TIM BERNERS-LEE (196)

How Diversity Works

If we believe diversity is critical in a fast-paced world of continuous innovation and change, can it be measured and how does it work? There are many headlines reporting that companies with diverse workforces and diverse management teams outperform competitors that do not. Research also found "diversity unlocks innovation and drives market growth" (197) increases revenues and accesses more customers. Financial successes are reported including higher profits, and ease of attracting more diverse talents (198). Employee satisfaction is improved when people see like-minded role models and company image enhanced with better social responsibility (106, 199).

Yet the question remains – what is the link? Diversity is proven to impact business performance through positive behaviours. First and foremost, making better decisions. Diversity prompts people to analyze facts, think more deeply and develop their own opinions. It improves the way people think and therefore generates better conclusions and results (200). This is why diversity is critical in a fast-paced world of continuous innovation and change!

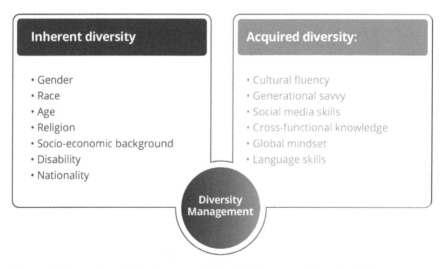

Figure 62: Examples of the Characteristics of Inherent and Acquired Diversity

In the context of companies, the term diversity signifies the differences and similarities of the workforce due to inherent or acquired characteristics. Both are important and both areas can be managed.

The value of inherent diversity can include customer focus, for example, when at least one member of a team has the same traits as the customer, this customer type is better understood by the whole team. (197).

According to the McKinsey report "Diversity Matters" (106), companies with a **culturally diverse workforce are more successful**. And while greater gender and ethnic diversity in corporate leadership doesn't automatically translate into more profit, there is a correlation – companies which commit themselves to diverse leadership are better able to win top talent and improve their customer orientation, employee satisfaction, and decision making. All that leads to a cycle of increasing returns and therefore more success (106).

Success Factors for a Diverse Workforce

Creating and retaining a diverse workforce is not about simply "adding" under-represented groups.

Firstly, good people are attracted to winning companies so business success counts.

Secondly, the environment and working conditions are important for all people and values of inclusiveness should drive policies to ensure many employees, especially in dual roles with career and household responsibility, remain in the workforce. Here data shows women especially join or leave companies for work-life balance and more women leave companies due to politics and the "men's club" (199).

Thirdly, the opportunity for career development must be transparent and fair for all employees. Sales Force CEO Marc Benioff (201), a vocal advocate for diversity, highlights a key belief that development investments should be for everyone, in other words, gender neutral opportunities and **developing talents** from within, are fundamental for a paradigm shift.

Finally, challenging and removing unconscious bias in managers is essential, a point also noted by Benioff. Unconsciously, we tend to like people who look like us, think like us, come from backgrounds similar to ours. Research shows that beliefs and values gained from family, culture and life experiences heavily influence how we view and evaluate both others and ourselves. This effect can have massive impact on managers hiring and promoting decisions if they are not actively taking their own unconscious bias into account.

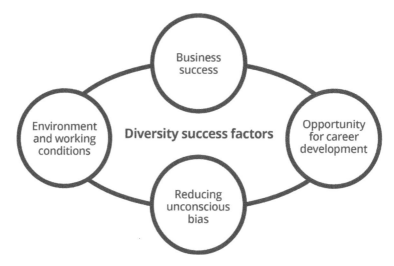

Figure 63: Success Factors for Diversity and Inclusion in the Workplace

If we look at all the people we know, there are different **levels of trust** (202):

- The wider "community" is all people we get to know, know their names, meet them more than once and this group shows the highest level of diversity yet the lowest level of trust based on a transactional nature and norms of the context of the relationship.
- Next are people we know better, have lunch with etc... A relationship moves from the "community" into the "crowd" by demonstration of trustworthy behaviour over time, where parties can reliably predict each other's behaviour. This is the group where we would typically find relationships with team members, co-workers, or associates.
- Lastly, the "core" are people we turn to when there is an interesting project, even promotion, or to represent ourselves or teams. There is often the least amount of diversity here as these are people who tend to think similarly to how we think ourselves.

There is nothing wrong with this and it is natural; people get along well with people who are similar to them, share the same values, experiences and backgrounds. This makes us feel safe, comfortable, get agreement and reassurance in our own identity. The scientific term for this behavior is **similarity attraction** (203) or "love of the same" – which means the tendency of individuals to associate and bond with similar people. Many studies have shown this effect, be it in friendships, partnerships, or also in the professional environment. In the business world however, we need to consider what impact this has on teams and organizations. If we surround ourselves with people similar to ourselves, this influences the way we see the world, what we evaluate as being good, bad, right, wrong. It narrows our mind, and our options. Becoming aware of this gives more opportunities to act differently in the future!

We referred to unconscious bias in chapter 6, when we consider the psychology of first impressions. **Unconscious bias** (105) relates to the mental "shortcuts" our brain takes based on personal experiences and stereotypes. Unconscious biases are the automatic, mental shortcuts used to process information and make decisions quickly (106). At any given moment individuals are flooded with information yet can only consciously process about 40 items. Cognitive filters and heuristics allow the mind to unconsciously prioritize, generalize, and dismiss large volumes of input. These shortcuts can be useful when making decisions with limited information, focus, or time, but can sometimes lead individuals astray and have unintended consequences in the workplace. For example, in important decisions, such as recruiting or promoting, they can mislead and limit new approaches. Unconscious bias can prevent individuals from making objective decisions, overlook great ideas, undermine individual potential, as well as create a less than ideal work experience for other colleagues. It is therefore important to know that background, personal experiences, societal stereotypes and cultural context can have an impact on decisions and actions without realising it.

Scientists have shown that such stereotypes begin to form early in childhood to serve a purpose for simplification. Clustering people into groups with expected traits does help navigate the world without being overwhelmed by information. The downside is that the potential for prejudice is hard-wired into human cognition.

However, at the individual level, the extent to which such biases are internalised and acted on varies widely and in complex ways. If leaders are aware of these associations, they can bring to bear all critical skills and intelligence to see the risks and overcome them. Through learning and reflection, leaders can discover how to best deal with the unconscious bias that limits diversity and define actions to decrease the influence such biases might have on their team and performance. This can also include actively seeking second opinions and use of technology, such as using algorithms in recruiting processes.

'Strength lies in differences, not in similarities'

STEPHEN COVEY (151)

How to Challenge Personal Unconscious Biases

Once aware of unconscious biases, let's consider what can be done in order to avoid being influenced by them. Not falling into the "unconscious bias trap", however can be quite difficult, but concepts from Daniel Kahnemann, Winner of the Nobel Prize 2002 in Economic Sciences and "inventor of the unconscious bias" can help. In his bestseller "Thinking, Fast and Slow" he differentiates two modes of thought (204):

- "system 1" is fast, instinctive and emotional
- "system 2" is slower, more deliberative, and more logical.

Unconscious biases are part of the "system 1" type of thinking, which makes them very effective, but not thought-through. Learning to use system 2 more, can enable rational thinking and decision making.

1. **Reconsidering important information** – Linked to effective decision making, as described in the competency of decision making and touched upon in chapter 5, decisions taken must be within our authority and ability. Decisions need to be timely yet must consider relevant information and this may also mean taking more time to reconsider the reasons, actively challenging biases, seeking new perspectives from others and then reviewing options, alternative solutions and consequences. This may prompt corrections. Finally, decisions must be communicated well. A good time to consider such logical decision making is when hiring a new employee to avoid affinity, anchoring and confirmation biases.

2. **Examining assumptions** – One difficulty is that in our imagination, when we think about problems or reaching goals, we form patterns. These patterns are self-imposed boundaries or barriers, that keep our thinking in a framework. We constrain our own thinking in this way (189). This "box" in our head represents our assumptions and we all have assumptions about the way something is or the way something should be. So, thinking outside the box is another term for examining and challenging our assumptions and judgements we make every day. Having a closer look at these assumptions helps to avoid being guided by them. Examples for assumptions are: "She has two small kids, she won't have time to be involved in the project"; "He is an IT person. He's probably not the best person to solve this conflict. We need someone with strong communication skills"; "He is an introvert. I doubt, he'll be a good leader". A leader must question these assumptions and also challenge employees to think outside the box in their head (as highlighted above). The next time you catch yourself making a judgement about a person's background or working style, stop and ask yourself, if this attribute could also be an asset instead!

3. **Paying attention to micro-behaviours** – Micro-behaviours are the tiny little things we do every day, which make another person feel appreciated, respected and included – or not. These are examples for micro-behaviours: Looking at someone, while they are talking, maybe nodding in agreement – instead of looking at your phone; Acknowledging the idea someone had – instead of showing no reaction; Greeting someone with a handshake, saying their name and establishing eye contact – instead of saying "hello" without looking at the person. Observe your micro-behaviours. Which ones do you use when talking to a person you feel comfortable with? Which of these could you also use with a person you normally don't feel connected with? Feeling genuinely appreciated lifts people up, makes people feel safe, which frees them up to do their best work. Feeling valued also helps avoid conflict. According to Paul McGee (87), conflict may stem from many reasons such as not being listened to, being overlooked or not consulted, yet the core impact is the same – people not feeling important. "Treating someone in a way that is unique to them is a powerful way to make that person feel important" and appreciated.

4. **Creating an environment for innovation** – As discussed above, leaders must actively seek ways to involve everyone, asking each member to contribute and asking for expert inputs. They must also give people time to formulate ideas and ignore conventions and boundaries to welcome open contributions from all sides.

5. **Building heterogeneous teams** – Homogeneous teams may be easy to manage yet can also result in no new ideas coming to the table and focus remains only on what is already known. All customers will not be represented and different perspectives simply missing. When hiring, promoting, assigning projects and developing, great leaders actively prioritise diversity. However, a common viewpoint often quoted is "I just want the best person for the job". Diversity and ability are not mutually exclusive! Diversity is an added benefit to augment attitude, skills and experience. Though many managers may feel safer hiring people just like them, as they believe they know what they will get, team performance will suffer long term. To build a more dynamic and successful team, when looking to hire, establish project teams or promote people into new positions, defining clear requirements for roles is paramount. This way, each candidate can be evaluated using the requirements, which makes the decision more objective and less prone to biases. The result of heterogeneous teams is success, through enhanced decision making, optimized efficiency, quality and innovation.

This challenge of personal bias is also mirroring what leaders can do to establish a better thinking environment for others and ensuring others value the connectedness of working together. Though the paradigm shift required for such fully inclusive organizations requires many active changes including mind sets, policies, procedures and systems, individual leaders can make a difference every day. Diversity won't happen on its own. Leaders who stand up and make a difference will see the difference in their results. And diversity at senior management levels really does matter! For example, not only does lack of gender diversity at senior levels influence perception of opportunities for other women to progress (205, 206), in many industries, financial performance is worse when there are no women at executive level. Overall, all types of diversity bring better decision making and as a leader, empowering people to think and leveraging the power of diversity means choosing to hire, promote, develop and value different people with different perspectives. The impact on business results however is remarkable (206):

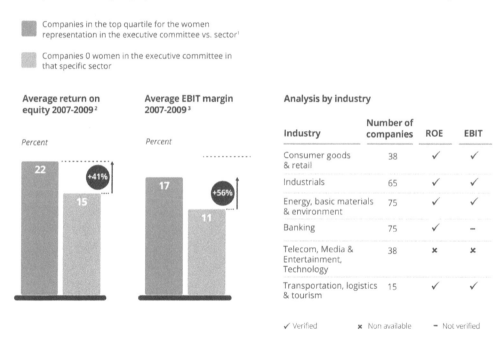

Companies with a higher proportion of women in their executive committees have better financial performance

Companies in the top quartile for the women representation in the executive committee vs. sector[1]

Companies 0 women in the executive committee in that specific sector

Average return on equity 2007-2009[2]

Average EBIT margin 2007-2009[3]

Analysis by industry

Industry	Number of companies	ROE	EBIT
Consumer goods & retail	38	✓	✓
Industrials	65	✓	✓
Energy, basic materials & environment	75	✓	✓
Banking	75	✓	−
Telecom, Media & Entertainment, Technology	38	✗	✗
Transportation, logistics & tourism	15	✓	✓

✓ Verified   ✗ Non available   − Not verified

Figure 64: Example Data on Impact of Gender Diversity on Business Results (206)

'If you do not intentionally include,
you unintentionally exclude'

NEIL LENANE (207)

In summary, the fourth I of the **extended Transformational Leadership model**, "intellectual stimulation" is describing new thinking and the benefits of all employees engaged in problem solving and creative thinking. To bring this concept further to life, here are examples of actions from highly successful global leaders.

What Intellectual Stimulation Looks Like in Practice

"To provide intellectual stimulation, I strongly believe in giving freedom to operate. People in my team have always been able to work from home or part time or in any other sort of agile and flexible context (even on leadership level which has been questioned by some of my colleagues' multiple times). I have been rewarded with a lot of wonderful and innovative ideas and a very high level of motivation and performance". *Thomas Schweins, Senior Vice President, QIAGEN.*

"This is the fun bit, challenging people to think, even provoking thoughts when required, to shake up the dynamics and see just what a team is capable of". *Peer M. Schatz.*

"An associate came back recently from a training course on agile management methods (scrum foundation) and was very enthusiastic. We wanted to reward and share this energy and gave him a presentation slot in our senior management team meeting with which he normally doesn't have much interaction. He is now known to the senior management as someone with added skills and who can be approached and asked for advice." *Heiko Kühne, VP Cosmetics & Chemicals Business, OPTIMA packaging group GmbH.*

"If leaders don't push diversity, groupthink will occur! Heterogeneous teams are key, bringing very different people together. And not all will like it, yet it has to happen for business success". *Peer M. Schatz.*

"We have created a cross functional innovation team for new technology development. The team has defined its mission, built their own dedicated room and has large freedom to operate". *Joachim Dittrich, Chairman OPTIMA Consumer Division, OPTIMA packaging group GmbH.*

"Even within HR, 50% of jobs as we know them today will have disappeared in 10 years' time through technology and application of artificial intelligence. Therefore, the skill sets associated with flexibility and agile working are key to be able to adapt and innovate and re-create. All managers need to step back and allow their teams to think, to discuss "crazy ideas", see what works in other settings and be willing to try new things. Simple steps in meetings to add a "creative thinking" agenda point

can remind everyone to take the time to think and not always do the same old…"
Alison Staley, HR Consultant and Chartered Fellow of Chartered Institute of Personnel and Development.

Key Learning Points

- Empowering people to think must be active and consider barriers / hindrances that need to be removed
- It is a primary responsibility of leaders to include people in planning, problem solving and decision making, as well as encouraging them to develop creative ideas and solutions on their own and for their own area of responsibility
- Challenging the status quo means seeking better ways, considering new options, examining assumptions, overcoming "norms" and thinking beyond the boxes of our minds
- Mistakes will happen, key is what we learn from them
- Innovation can only occur when groupthink stops, and all voices are heard. The climate for innovation must include less rules, risk taking and experimentation
- Diverse teams and diverse perspectives are the best way to achieve better thinking, more insights, improved decision making and superior performance
- Achieving diversity and inclusion in the workplace starts from talented people wanting to work in a winning business and then staying due to an inclusive environment / conditions (policies and culture), plus fair opportunity for career development
- Removal of unconscious bias is essential across an organization to leverage the power of diversity
- Hiring for and promoting diversity should be a must for any transformational leader

Personal Reflection Points

Question 1: How do you empower people to think? Give examples.

Question 2: How well do you facilitate meetings / workshops? Be honest – do you always give your opinion first? Remember, this will always stifle creativity and inputs from others.

Question 3: When was the last time you "celebrated" failure and used it as a learning experience?

Question 4: How well do you embrace diversity? Take a sheet of paper and write down 10 names of people in your team or people you trust most from your professional environment or close friends (not family). Done? Now draw 7 columns and label: gender, race/ethnicity, age, sexual orientation, education, disability y/n, marital status – and fill them in for each person.

Now look at your list – if you are anything like most people, it will be a pretty homogeneous list and similar to yourself in your core circle of trust…. What can you learn here?

Chapter 11
Including Everyone and Everything

Key Knowledge...

- The 5th I, integrative support, describes the additional connectedness required in the new digital age

Key Actions...

- Build and maintain long term relations, despite distance or virtual environments
- Create team spirit and collaborative teamwork across fragmented groups
- Active personal and team-focused networking
- Leverage a digital mind set

Impacts...

- Leaders able to meet global demands and lead effectively outside face-to-face situations
- Leaders as new role models in the digital age, embracing and leveraging technology for competitive advantage
- Access to and impact on global resources including customers, suppliers, collaborators, networks and employees

Transformational Leadership, well documented over many years, is a winning style and proven to deliver higher satisfaction, motivated employees, and overall better business performance. It is also well documented in complex and rapidly changing environments. Though even this model needs updating in the digital era and here we will explain the new 5th I, **integrative support** (29). As reviewed in chapter 1, the opportunities brought about by globalization and digitalization are immense for businesses, yet these do bring with them challenges for leaders in terms of how to include everyone and how to leverage technology to simply remain connected, as well as maximise output. This theme of integration, despite location or distance, is core to this new 5th I of transformational leadership.

Building and Maintaining Long Term Relationships: Leading Virtual Teams

In the digital age, transformational leaders need to expand beyond face-to-face leadership, into successful leadership of remote and virtual teams, including home workers. The personal challenges of this increased distance are significant; not only does a leader have reduced direct influence on remote teams, leaders must also learn to embrace new technologies to connect with people. The increased physical distance and virtual interactions between leaders and their employees must be understood and managed well. Stress is placed on leaders to spend more time reaching out to team members and being more available, to build two-way trust and connect with individuals.

So how to build and maintain **long term employee relationships**, despite distance? Actions to connect with others include:

1. Recognizing the employees' strengths, development areas and individual needs is critical for leaders to set meaningful and challenging goals based on ability of the individual to succeed, then empower and delegate effectively.
2. Mechanisms must also be established to facilitate employee meetings, performance reviews, goal monitoring, feedback and coaching. These may include face-to face meetings, as well as make use of digital solutions with cameras on, for frequent connections, in other words, deploying good virtual communication.
3. Time invested in getting to know employees is really critical. It is engaging not only in business talk, but also choosing to take the time to connect as people. Often interactions on the phone for example are stifled and leaders need to feel comfortable and get passed this hurdle.

Though this may be considered part of "Individual Consideration", in the context of a virtual team and less direct influence, more emphasis is placed on leaders' emotional competencies to build rapport and show sensitivity to the individual's needs. For the employee, distance reduces control and necessitates increased self-responsibility. Furthermore, lack of day to day interaction may contribute to uncertainty. Though a leader may have high ambiguity tolerance, they must be cognitive of the unsettling effect this may have on those under them, provide more information than before and again spend more time in dialogue.

Creating Spirit Across Fragmented Groups

The second significant change is creating **team spirit and collaborative teamwork** across fragmented groups. A transformational leader actively engages the team, ensures teams identify with organizational values and goals, and creates team spirit, a feeling of pride and loyalty. Yet in the context of Integrative Support, once again this is expanded to achieve a broader cooperative environment, specifically increased connectedness on a human level virtual collaboration. So, what's new?

1. The starting point for collaborative teamwork is still engaging the team with the organizational values and goals, because once trust and commitment are established, both virtual and face-to-face teams can achieve a state of mutual influence.
2. Mutual influence describes collaborative decision making, shared responsibility and team members leading others towards achievement of goals (208).

'The nice thing about teamwork is that you always have others on your side'

MARGARET CARTY (209)

Such steps can also be considered to fall under the banner of Inspirational Motivation, however in the virtual environment this must be actively augmented with the establishment of shared identity, a "we" feeling, and shared context to avoid social distance. Research also shows that leading virtual teams requires more leadership time and more structural supports for effective performance (208, 210). Leaders must therefore be mindful to leverage all transformational skills first and foremost to build trust, and secondly, take full responsibility for establishing formal structures for shared understanding or mutual knowledge. Transparent communication and information management, both of the work being done and the working environment, enable efficient coordination and collaboration, and alongside shared identity, avoid conflict.

With this increased teamwork and more scope and design for work content devolved to teams, again self-responsibility and team self-organization increases (36). Working successfully with others to achieve common goals, means all employees need to build constructive working relationships with co-workers and partners. As such, this also requires enhanced interpersonal adaptability, especially with team members in different locations or cultural differences.

It is also worth noting that such consideration applies equally well to project teams brought together for expertise, yet also requiring a clear goal, shared identity and knowledge on work and team members, to efficiently complete defined tasks before being disbanded. Project and virtual teams have many benefits (211) and virtual teams of remote workers and home workers are the future of workplace structure and culture. Firstly, it may make best sense to have remote employees close to customers, for example sales professionals, to maintain close business relationships. Virtual teams are often the best approach for companies who are looking to find the right talent and expertise, anywhere in the world. Such teams save organizations from the challenges and cost of setting up additional infrastructure in locations where they want a presence, but a physical office is not always needed. And though day to day management is more distant, performance tracking is within the organization's direct control, unlike some outsourcing models. There are benefits for employees too including flexibility, no relocation or transition related changes. This means employees are motivated and focused to deliver the results. Diverse remote teams utilize the huge potential of globalized business. Technology and globalisation have made it possible to make this a sustainable option, and for leaders with the transformational skills, it is a new opportunity to access a new world of business and talent whilst still creating meaningful relationships and effective collaborative teams to include everyone.

Utilizing Networks to Share Knowledge

Network-based work approaches have also gained increasing importance because of changes in global business, in workflows and in the work environment. Both internal and external collaborations are the new norm as businesses come to understand that growth and innovation cannot take place in a vacuum and require different points of view and diverse skill sets more rapidly. The requirement is now for a leader to utilize both personal and team-focused networking to gain access to new knowledge and unlock the potential of diverse thinking and innovation, through collaboration. For individuals, connecting with others in networks and gaining new insights is clearly an opportunity and this is type of activity is familiar to most successful leaders. However, the next step for leaders is to promote networking amongst their teams and this requires trust. Encouraging employees to join external networks especially means employees understanding why they are there, what they can and cannot share, and how they can leverage their new insights in a productive way.

So why is this all happening and why is the work environment increasingly characterized by a feeling of cooperation and interconnectedness and virtual collaboration? An important reason is the Internet and phenomena such as Facebook (212). With over a billion users, Facebook has changed the social life of our species and evidence shows its use to connect people with specialist interests, sharing information and experiences. This rise in networking, the exchange of ideas among individuals or groups that share a common interest, will continue. The digital business also uses all forms of interconnectedness, leveraging technology to enable collaboration with colleagues, customers, partners, suppliers and experts across the globe.

*'The nature of humans is that they
need to build alliances'*

HARLEY LOVEGROVE (184)

As a new element for transformational leadership in the digital age, networking establishes mutually beneficial relationships to exchange ideas and build knowledge. This exchange of information includes leaders actively seeking new ideas or broader perspectives from within an organization or from outside. Other benefits are (213):

• New contacts – Meeting potential clients or identifying opportunities for partnerships, joint ventures, or new areas of expansion for the business.
• Visibility – Communicating with partners on a regular basis to maintain business relationships.
• Staying current – Keeping up with market conditions and overall industry trends.
• Problem solving – Finding solutions to business problems or needs, including finding candidates for roles or investment.
• Confidence and morale – a boost from spending time with optimistic and successful people.

Another benefit of networking, both formal and informal, that is accelerated by the internet, is **collective learning**. Collective learning is the ability to share information so efficiently that the ideas of individuals can be stored within the collective memory of communities and can accumulate. In the workplace, knowledge sharing behaviours: consuming, connecting, creating and contributing knowledge, are associated with collective learning practices. All of this sharing is accelerated by use of the internet. Evidence also shows that "intensely networked and communicating groups have a much faster learning curve and develop more innovative solutions. Such groups quickly create innovations that lead to novel business models, methods and ways of working. This combination of creative minds and worldwide networking is the basis for a wave of innovations and transformation of business models" (214).

Leaders as Role Models for Networking: Effective networking should also look at its purpose. There are three defined forms of networkers; operational, focused on current work, mainly with internal contacts; personal, focused on professional development with external contacts; and strategic, considering future priorities, bringing new insights, industry trends and enabling leaders to stay current with market conditions and best practices. Once again, the networks described can be informal or formal. However, studies found most leaders who think they are adept at networking often operate at an operational or personal level and only highly effective leaders learn to employ networks for strategic purposes (215). The difference lies in mind set, believing that networking is one of the most important requirements of a senior role, and allocating enough time and effort to see it pay off.

Within an organization, expectations of a leader therefore include role modelling networking activities; involving external experts for improvements, visibly engaging with thought-leaders and including team members in networks. By leading by example, this could be considered Idealized Influence, however, the added focus needs to be on encouraging team member participation in internal and external networks for further insights, as well as leaders taking a more active online presence to share knowledge. For employees, not only do they need to understand the value, they also need to reallocate time to benefit from networking, as well as showing initiative, seeking diverse perspectives.

Online Visibility: Another new topic for leaders in the digital age is the utilization of technologies for active sharing and presence in the online world of social media. Today, with many leaders choosing to produce social media content, write blogs, use twitter etc, the opportunity to share knowledge and experience via such channels is exciting, offering new reach and spread of information. There are many reasons why leaders should be active and visible online and make it a priority (216, 217):

- Positioning themselves and the company as experts – According to a Brandfog Report 2014, 82% of people believe that executive-level engagement on social media demonstrates industry expertise and leadership.
- Earning the trust of others – According to an Adweek Survey 2013, more than 80% of customers are more likely to trust a company whose CEO and leadership team are active on these channels.
- Engaging with customers using social media uses personal channels, communicating the more human side of the business.
- Attracting the best talent – Four out of five employees believe that CEOs who engage on social media are better equipped to lead companies in the modern world (Adweek Survey)

- Setting a good example – According to an article by Paul Dunay (218), content shared by employees on social media drives eight times more engagement than content shared via brand channels.
- Adding wider value – One of the most enriching consequences of digital engagement is the opportunity to influence the environment better. Companies don't operate in isolation and the online world provides opportunity to support ideas, values and initiatives aligned with company goals.

'Embracing social media isn't just a bit of fun, it's a vital way to communicate, keep your ear to the ground and improve your business'

RICHARD BRANSON (219)

Finally, as businesses do come to the realisation that innovation especially cannot take place in a vacuum, unique collaborations and industry networks are springing up to increase the probabilities of innovation success (220). This co-innovation, introduced in chapter 10, is an example of network-based intellectual stimulation, leads firms to collaborate with their customers, partners, and other stakeholders. Benefits have included new commercial opportunities, increased chances of creating more new products and services that are successful, reduced overall cost of developing new products or services so improving a business's financial performance. Surprising networks have been seen outside traditional industry boundaries. Examples include Google's first partnership with a major automaker, to test self-driving technology or the joint venture between Intel and BMW to develop self-driving systems. Audi, BMW and Daimler, traditional competitors, spent $3 billion in partnership to purchase Here's digital mapping services to jointly compete against Google Maps. All these formal network collaborations are great examples of the changing face of business and the need to share knowledge when there is a strong shared interest to do so.

In the digital age, leaders have more possibilities to access and make use of networks for both themselves and their teams. Unlocking this potential of networks includes accessing knowledge, diversity and ultimately innovation.

Embracing a Digital Mind Set

Thinking digitally to achieve connectedness is critical in today's business world with digital transformation a strategic focus for many organizations. The challenge however is many leaders are not as technically up to date or comfortable with fast technological advances. Though a leader does require high levels of digital competence to understand and apply technology, this is more in the context of facilitating business goals, rather than the digital expertise required by specialists creating IT infrastructure or digital content. The key focus for leaders is therefore a digital mind set and openness to exploit technology for business competitiveness (51, 52).

It is clear from looking at the rate of change in society and business that digital competence is required by everyone, meaning the ability to find, evaluate and contribute information using digital platforms. European Union reports describe digital competence as a "set of knowledge, skills and attitudes … that are required when using information communication technology and digital media" (221) and these skills and knowledge refer to abilities associated with data literacy, communication, collaboration, as well as content creation, safety and technical problem solving (222).

'Digital isn't a software; it's a mind set'

AARON DIGNAN (223)

A digital mind set sees and actively makes use of the opportunities coming with new technologies. Whether a company successfully manages the digital transformation does not depend initially on introducing the right technologies. First and foremost, it's about the digital mind set of the leaders, which is why it is not about the software. This also means facilitating the technical know-how of teams and provision of infrastructure, flexible access and enabling information flow.

Defining a digital strategy must also sit with leaders, alongside the commitment to technology, yet linked to intellectual stimulation, encouraging employee creativity with technology to improve tasks, relationships and results is only part of the shift. Stimulating people to change the way they approach business problems and where they look to find solutions is also central to digital transformation. Technology can aid work access and make communication easier with virtual teams and networks.

Though belief in technology can be a business lever, commitment from leaders to invest and make rapid changes is also necessary, as is the willingness and ability across the entire workforce. Such redefined expectations for employees extend beyond digital competencies and necessitate employees to show more personal flexibility and openness to new perspectives and for teams to develop better collaborative abilities. Understanding these new requirements for employees is important to define the profile of an ideal candidate for this new environment, including workers proficient in digital competencies, as well as those able to work in flexible structures and networks, and able to succeed in virtual environments. These can be hired for and developed. Details of these are covered in chapter 12.

Leadership constitutes a complex interaction between leaders, employees, and the context in which they operate. Leading transformationally in the digital age requires leaders to demonstrate all 5 Is, bringing Idealized influence, Inspirational motivation, Individual consideration, Intellectual stimulation and Integrative support. Doing so will enable businesses and teams to navigate the digital revolution and globalization that are changing the way of work today and tomorrow. This will also engage employees and transform them to a higher level of performance (46).

In summary, the fifth I of the **extended Transformational Leadership model**, "integrative support" is adding how to connect even more in our digital and global world. Again, it is not just about technology but also the mind set of inclusiveness. To bring this final concept further to life, here are examples of actions from highly successful global leaders.

What Integrative Support Looks Like in Practice

"Creating team spirit is all about 'we're in this together'. For me, this is where the tool 'DISC' provides guidance and the appreciation to understand each team members' strengths and how each person works and communicates. We're not all good at everything, so we need to acknowledge that and then work as a team to use the individual strengths to achieve goals together." *Alison Staley, HR Consultant and Chartered Fellow of Chartered Institute of Personnel and Development.*

"We've tried to not only agree on plans and project via email, but use video conference technology to connect the team. Afterwards all agree it improved the emotional buy in". *Heiko Kühne, VP Cosmetics & Chemicals Business, OPTIMA packaging group GmbH.*

"Stimulating the social interaction, the informal discussions, is important in virtual environments, however maintaining the professional framework is also essential. For instance, on video calls, it means no washing machines in the background, a suitable backdrop and work attire". *Peer M. Schatz.*

"To build and maintain a strong team spirit I believe it is important to balance regular virtual team meetings with the possibility to meet as a global team once or twice a year as this helps to strengthen the bond. I have always stressed meeting discipline to keep the team spirit and performance up. A regular team meeting has always been the most important priority. You can only not attend if you are on holiday or off sick." *Thomas Schweins, Senior Vice President, QIAGEN.*

"As a response to the Corona virus crisis we established daily Skype and video calls to respond to the changing situation and discuss measures. Opening the sessions with senior leaders sets the tone and improves the atmosphere of the calls". *Joachim Dittrich, Chairman OPTIMA Consumer Division, OPTIMA packaging group GmbH.*

Key Learning Points

- The reality of globalization and new ways of working means most leaders will have to influence employees, customers, suppliers or networks outside their own physical location and these virtual partners must be connected with

- Virtual team leadership requires much more thought, effort, systems and communication tools to reduce effects of distance, build trust and create a sense of belonging

- Collaborations continue to increase in relevancy and technology can be leveraged for all aspects of project work

- Networking to share knowledge is a manifestation of the new knowledge, digital and global era. Not only do network interactions consume our private lives, they can enhance access to people, resources, knowledge and intellectual stimulation

- Leaders need to be visible in networks and encourage their teams to do so too; this includes online presence for reach and positioning

- To achieve connectedness in the digital age, leaders are not required to be technology experts but must understand and leverage technology for business success. This digital mind set includes ensuring the right technology is available for employees, alongside their willingness and ability to use it

Personal Reflection Points

Question 1: How do you use technology to connect everyone and everything? Give examples of tools such as for analysis, planning, knowledge management, people management, customer management and communication.

Question 2: How do you leverage technology for enhancing developing and maintaining relationships with global partners or virtual workers?

Question 3: What networks are you active in? How can you encourage others to network more?

Chapter 12
A Few Words of Caution

Key Knowledge...

- The complexity of business also requires leaders to consider the appropriateness of any leadership approach and show adaptability when necessary

Key Actions...

- Acknowledge that new competencies are required by leaders *and* employees
- Hire and develop for new employee competencies in the digital age
- Continue to treat employees as individuals and adopt appropriate leadership styles to enable all to succeed
- Engage in personal life-long learning

Impacts...

- Highly effective leaders, situationally appropriate
- Skilled, competent and engaged employees
- An organization fit for the global and digital business world

It is clear that as demands change on leaders in the digital age, to be led transformationally in the digital age also redefines expectations and competencies for employees as well. This impact on employees must be understood to ensure the right abilities are hired for and developed. It is also essential that leaders themselves reflect on their teams and the current team make-up for effectiveness.

New Employee Competencies in the Digital Age

In addition to important digital competencies including knowledge of digital system technologies, skills to be proficient in the use of technology and a digital mind set (221, 222), new employee competencies must also be considered for success. Requirements are for employees to show more personal flexibility and openness to new perspectives and for teams to develop better collaborative abilities. Such new competencies therefore cover new aspects of self-management, relationship management and mental agility and can be seen here:

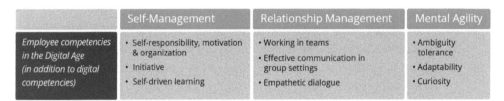

	Self-Management	Relationship Management	Mental Agility
Employee competencies in the Digital Age (in addition to digital competencies)	• Self-responsibility, motivation & organization • Initiative • Self-driven learning	• Working in teams • Effective communication in group settings • Empathetic dialogue	• Ambiguity tolerance • Adaptability • Curiosity

Figure 65: Examples of New Employee Competencies Required in the Digital Age and when Working Remotely

Self-Management: With the workplace changes described that result in increased distance between leader and employee, the requirement for increased **self-management and discipline** is evident. This will include self-responsibility for behaviour, self-motivation to achieve goals and self-organization of tasks and time. **Initiative** and **self-driven learning** will also ensure self-directed work process improvements and iterative personal development. Overall, less control and risk of more limited feedback means employees must demonstrate self-sufficiency and accountability for individual performance and business results.

Relationship Management: The increasing collaborative nature of work today and the connectedness that brings, means all employees must demonstrate high ability for teamwork. **Working in teams** will include constructively working with people of different departments and cultures and across distances, to achieve common goals. It will require building constructive relationships, characterized by high levels of acceptance, trust, cooperation and mutual respect. Liaising with others concerning the completion of tasks will also challenge people to consider group dynamics, collective decision making and a more active and cooperative approach to planning and problem solving. This also mirrors the leader's need for a digital mind set, leveraging technology to allow for collaboration in the workplace in a way to bring in different experiences and new ways of viewing any situation. Finally, as collaboration must be inclusive, extended demands will be placed on employees' **communication skills**, both in the digital context but also in group settings. Purposefully using multiple channels or means to ensure an efficient information flow, whilst considering the communication which is most appropriate for the situation and target group will be necessary. Employees will also have to demonstrate more **empathetic dialogue**, listen actively and asks questions to build rapport and avoid misunderstandings; furthermore, respectfully addressing discrepancies and conflict will also ensure more effective group dynamics and synergistic outcomes.

Mental Agility: With faster rates of business change combined with less direct control, more pressure will be placed on employees to deal with uncertainty. **Ambiguity tolerance**, the ability to handle uncertainty, lack of structure and to make decisions and change comfortably, will become more and more paramount. However, when missing, a person may become anxious or try to add structure or controls. Accepting new ways of working and **adapting** to change are fundamental to achieving a new mindset shift. The digital landscape is ever-changing, and employees will need to adapt with these changes. However, an individual's inclination to adapt to different circumstances and modify their behaviours can vary and may be hindered by lack of maturity. Finally, to go beyond current thinking, tasks and roles, **curiosity** is key. Intellectual curiosity gives the inner desire for a deeper understanding and enables ever more interconnected possibilities (184). Seizing all opportunities and exploring new concepts, new perspectives, new ideas and new solutions may be a step outside the comfort zone yet a step in the right direction towards innovation.

It is well established that competencies are transferable abilities enabling success in complex and unknown situations and relevant to a wide range of work settings (56) and as such the overview above can be considered appropriate to facilitate agility and flexibility on the part of many types of organizations. Competencies are also learnable so can be developed by many employees, however the suggested competencies for the digital age are more akin to leader competencies (57) and less like individual contributor requirements. In addition, many may also be more attitudinal than skill based. The challenge here is that attitude is more difficult to change. Therefore, to lead transformationally and to achieve a digital transformation, the questions arise: is it possible to achieve such a paradigm shift in an existing team? And can all employees be led transformationally?

Can All Employees Be Led Transformationally?

Leadership must be relevant and adapted to the world in which the business occurs. What works well in one situation doesn't always have the same positive effect in another. Differences include constant disruptive change, global impacts such as cultural differences and dealing with individuals with differing needs and interests. A good leader needs to reflect the outside world and be appropriate for the team they are leading.

Balanced Engagement: A study at University of East Anglia, UK (224) looked at the relationship between presenteeism, transformational leadership, and the rate of absence related to sickness. Researchers found transformational leaders, who inspire their employees and team members to perform better at work, increased the risk of health complications and absence due to illness. These leaders pushed for longer hours and more commitment to work and employees, who wanted to make a good impression and were genuinely excited about work, were reluctant to take a sick day when they first showed signs of illness then infected others and the entire group lost more productivity as a result. The leaders also stoked perfectionist tendencies in their employees. And while perfectionism might help detail-orientation, it has a negative effect on mental and physical wellbeing in the long run. Such high expectations by leaders must be balanced.

On the flip side, another challenge may occur when employees loose belief over time. A leader needs to continually reinforce the vision and empower others to do their utmost to achieve it; however, if an employee begins to feel that their part is not important, they will lose interest (225). To maintain enthusiasm, employees need frequent feedback on progress made and their part in it. Therefore, maintaining engagement long term requires ongoing reinforcement of achievement, as well as strong intrinsic motivation to keep going.

Maturity of Employees: As transformational leadership is a process that occurs between employees and leaders, taking into consideration both persons involved and their individual needs (13), this means the leader must be aware of the individual motives of team members. However, common motivators such as affiliation or appreciation (23) may not motivate all employees all the time. Though personal congratulations rank at the top of motivators by many employees (152), gratitude is an attainment associated with emotional maturity (154).

The modern business environment itself may also introduce complexity regarding the profile of a successful remote or virtual worker. Randy Conley, Vice President of The Ken Blanchard Companies, noted that in their experience with clients, not everyone was cut out to be a successful virtual worker (226). They also suggested that the ideal personal profile included discipline, maturity, good time management skills as defined in the competency table (see figure 3 above), plus a successful track record of performance in the particular role.

Millennials: Where does that leave transformational leadership in the digital age with millennials? The millennial generation, also referred to as generation Y, is generally considered to be those born between 1981 and 1996. With some variations globally, this age group makes up almost 20% of the world's population and 15% of the global workforce (227). In the USA, millennials already contribute 35% of the workforce, and predicted to rise to 75% by 2030 (228). The challenge however is that millennials, as a group of people, are tough to manage (229). Not only can they be considered to lack maturity and have limited work experience based on age, data shows they change jobs more frequently than other generations. With limited proven track records and immaturity, virtual working may not be ideal. Simon Sinek also accuses millennials of being entitled, narcissistic, self-interested, unfocused and lazy, not the characteristics required by employees in the digital age (229). On the plus side, this group has a more positive attitude towards technology (230), they value high-trust cultures and seek jobs with purpose and meaning (231), all of which fits well with extended transformational leadership in the digital age. Key to successfully leading millennials therefore may come from application of transformational leadership, especially leveraging the core concept of the individual. At companies where leaders show sincere interest in millennials as people, organizations have seen an eight times improvement in agility and seven times increases in innovation (231). Millennial concern for long-term employability (232) also aligns with development goals of transformational leaders and if leveraged with defined steps to build a track record, may provide a stronger motive for enhancing performance and career development within one organization for a more sustainable period of time (119). Though with higher demands for feedback and recognition, leaders will have to be cognitive of "checking in" with millennials on a regular basis (232).

iGens: Also known as generation Z, these are people born 1995 onwards. These teens and young adults are vastly different from Millennials though their impact in the workplace is limited today. Studies (233) have shown that this group are highly tech-savvy having grown up with smart devices. They are also more tolerant, yet cautious, abhor inequality and are more likely to think for themselves. With role models such as Greta Thunberg and Malala Yousafzai, this generation may well be ready to shape change and create a more connected and purpose-driven environment too. Only time in the workplace will show.

Hiring for New Competencies within Younger Generations

Focusing back on the individual may also serve as an important reminder that studies on generational groups make conclusions on the group, with group behavioural tendencies and group values. As leaders, avoiding bias and stereotyping, and embracing diversity is proven to enhance team performance through better decision-making and therefore desirable (200). With competencies as known future performance indicators, it therefore makes sense when hiring and developing employees, especially millennials today and iGens over coming years, to target the employee competencies in the digital age, as descried in figure 3, to identify those able to succeed in a transformational environment.

Gender Differences?

Several studies over 20 years have shown that men and women value some of the same aspects of work but rank them differently (234, 235, 236). Men value pay and benefits, as well as power, authority, and status significantly more than women. Women value relationships, recognition and respect, communication, fairness and equity, teams and collaboration, family and home balance.

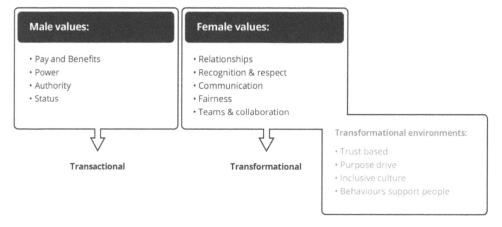

Figure 66: Examples of Gender Differences Related to Aspects Work Values

These male values may be considered more transactional, and the female more transformational. **Transactional** is a style of leadership that focuses on achieving results and goals by offering transactions: employees receive rewards for good performance, and they are punished by disciplinary actions in the case of poor performance (68, 73). There is also strong association with hierarchy and task orientation. This creates an environment focused on short term task delivery and is not inspirational or ideal long term or in complex worlds with constant change.

Our focus on a transformational environment, where leaders actively transform their employees to a higher level of performance is based around trust and individuals (45). It is also focused on organizational success, with employees actively included in business purpose, decisions and outcomes. It may however be considered too unstructured or too personally demanding for some employees.

Adapting Leadership Style

The impact of transformational leadership is well understood to be effective as it is active. When applying this approach, leaders actively transform their employees to a higher level of performance. As a style, it is considered the highest level on a continuum of styles with the level below being transactional leadership (53):

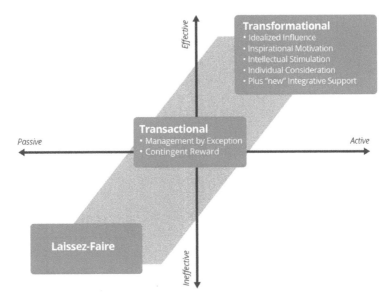

Figure 67: Representation of the Continuum of Leadership Styles

With transactional leadership, focus is on control and communication of expectations to achieve goals. It includes setting standards and monitoring outcomes (management by exception), however this is limited as focus on corrective actions means leaders are only heard from when things go wrong. It also includes exchanging reward and recognition for accomplishments; however, this can be perceived as too directive and hierarchic. To quote Kuhnert and Lewis (237), "transactional leaders are influential because it is in the best interest of subordinates for them to do what the leader wants." The limitations of transactional leadership are that it is not individualized to the needs of specific employees or specific situations, and it is not focused on personal development. Effort is on keeping up the existing status-quo and short-term achievement. While this may not work to motivate employees, it can work in environments with simple routine tasks, for employees who have a job to pay bills and no more, and may be necessary in a crisis where extreme clarity is required urgently. A well-known transactional leader was Bill Gates (238). He believed in the importance of clarity and was often described as a confrontational taskmaster however throughout the growth stages of Microsoft, his style contributed towards phenomenal success endorsing there is a time and place for such a style.

Although Laissez faire is considered to be the least effective, there are some positives associated with a more hands-off leadership approach: Employees have absolute freedom and are expected to solve problems with given resources. However, there are many more limitations that mean it is ineffective: No clear orientation or emphasis on results, little structure, no management of employee performance and no intervention when issues arise. All of this hinders individual and organizational performance long term. There are examples of such a passive style working for motivated teams with high expertise or creative teams valuing independence. A well-documented laissez faire leader was Warren Buffett, American business magnet. Buffett surrounded himself with people he knew could perform their tasks creatively and without his help and he would even allow mistakes for his people to learn from them. He did however limit failure by intervening when needed to correct unfavourable situations.

When describing the **continuum**, Bass argued that a leader does not have to decide between the two effective styles and that they build upon each other, with fair transactions establishing employees' trust (53). In the context of the digital age we argue that transformational leadership is best suited as it is focused on organizational success, includes employees in business purpose, and looks to develops employees. And as Bass also highlighted, "the more complex the environment and the tasks are, the higher the need for new ideas and innovations, and the faster the changes, the more important transformational leadership is" (53). However, leadership must reflect not only the business environment but also the employees. Employees who are led by a transformational leader put aside their immediate self-interests to the values, goals and interests of the organization. They need the shared values, ability and intrinsic motivation to do this. In a heterogeneous team, some employees with

	Leader Ability	Employee Ability
Transactional environment	Task oriented, goal setting, controlling	Meeting goals, implementing, following instructions
Transformational environment	+ Acting as a role model + Sharing a vision + Challenging the status quo + Acting with compassion + Collaborative	+ Self management + Relationship management + Mental agility

Figure 68: Summary of Abilities Required in Different Environments

high extrinsic motivation, or employees who simply see work to pay the bills, or those that struggle with complexity and change, or potentially Millennials, may feel overwhelmed. Managing such a team will require the leader to adapt and use a combination of both transformational and transactional styles to be more effective.

Leadership success is dependent on variable conditions, and as such, leaders will need to choose the right approach at the right time: When to focus on effectiveness and when to inspire others for a future vision. To achieve this the leader therefore needs:

- Insight to understand what is going on, when to change and what approach fits
- Flexibility to be able to move seamlessly from one style to another to meet the changing needs
- Ability to build trust and credibility and not to be seen as inconsistent
- Coaching skills to support others in their development
- Problem solving mind set to approach challenges in a solution-oriented manner to achieve best results.

As Colin Powell once said, "leadership is solving problems" (239) and an adaptive approach to leadership can be considered one such solution.

Leadership constitutes a complex interaction between leaders, employees, and the context in which they operate. As part of a **leader's development**, enhanced self-awareness of preferred styles and situational appropriateness, both environmental and towards employees, would allow for more reflection and actions to improve impact. Though transformational leadership will be paramount in the digital age, transformational leaders may require some finesse to deal with all employees for long term business success and enhanced ability to balance transactional and transformational leadership styles, especially in light of the ever-increasing globalization and digitalization changing all aspects of work for the global workforce.

Key Learning Points

- A transformational environment must consider not only leaders' abilities but also those of employees

- Transformational environments encourage commitment and performance especially in fast moving change and complexity. It requires effective infrastructure (technology), shared purpose (vision and values), strong management (strategy and structure) and strong leadership (5 Is)

- The agility gained through transformational leadership comes from employees also having abilities to self-manage, manage relationships and face ambiguity

- Virtual workers also require similar competencies, alongside discipline and maturity

- Not all employees will show high ambition or career motivation therefore hiring into a transformational environment requires hiring for key competencies or adapting a more transactional leadership approach for enhancing clarity when necessary

- Leaders should be able to balance transformational and transactional styles to be more situationally appropriate

Personal Reflection Points

Question 1: How would you describe your current working environment? What style of leadership best fits? How well can you adapt to people or business needs?

Question 2: When you are recruiting or promoting, what competencies do you look for in potential candidates? Do you need to review these in light of new employee competencies in the digital age?

Applying
Connectedness

Welcome to Part Four, where we consider how to apply connectedness in our changing world. Where impersonal technology, distance and excessive control risk engagement and inclusion, here we stress a new way with the importance of people and purpose for delivering sustainable and fulfilling business success.

Chapter 13
The Shift to Meaning

Key Knowledge...

- Purpose relates to a connection to something bigger than ourselves
- Connectedness is about connecting with self, others and the business
- Leading with purpose requires shared values, organizational vision, strong management and leadership principles described in the 5 Is

Key Actions...

- A personal shift from ego, to a new possibility of connectedness, growth and happiness
- Reaching out to others, building relationships and showing kindness
- Building resilience to manage the inevitable stresses of business

Impacts...

- Personal meaning
- Team engagement and commitment to organizational vision and values
- A transformational environment focused on organizational performance

A leader is responsible for the results of their team, project or area, yet leadership is not a title and in today's more egalitarian word, leadership is not about hierarchy. Leadership is about stepping forward, inspiring and motivating others to get involved and creating an environment in which all can succeed. With so much of our time invested in work, there is even more reason to make work fulfilling, both for those who choose to lead, as well as all those around them. Even the World Economic Forum highlighted a study in 2019, that concluded "relationships have the biggest effect on health" and the "importance of a good manager" and "skills to be a good manager" (240).

Work should no longer be about contracts, compliance and control (241). It should be about connectedness to what the organization stands for (8). The **transformational environment** describes an organization driven by shared purpose:

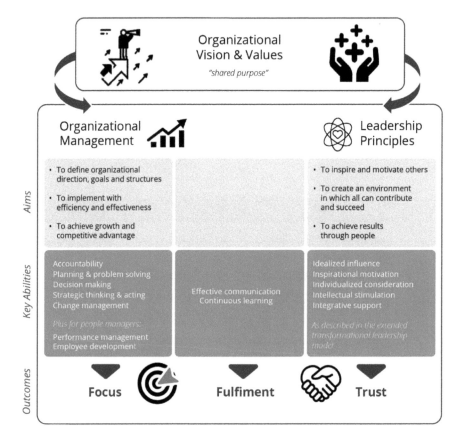

Figure 69: The Transformational Environment

Purpose relates to a connection to something bigger than ourselves. To lead with purpose requires letting go of ego and living and working with openness, honesty, humility and trust. These are big asks! Our societal norms and conditioned ambitions are highly linked to what we do, what we have, what "things" we achieve, how we compare to others, what we look like to others, what our reputation is etc. A shift to meaning and purpose requires letting go of the imagined order, the constructs we build and our personal egos (4). As a leader, it is simply forgetting self, choosing to connect with others and acting *for* others.

It starts by a shift in our personal **values**. Research has shown that when men are driven by ego and ambition, their top values relate to wealth, achieving and respect (4). It its slightly different for women with career, family and fitting in being important. However, for those that experience a shift to living by meaning and purpose, the values shift to connection, peace and family for men; growth, connection and happiness for women.

So now imagine an organization where people align such personal values with organizations values. This can be the new way or the new balance for business. It can define how we engage people's minds and nourish their souls. It then becomes about doing the right things for the organization (management) *and* doing them in the right way (leadership), for people to achieve extraordinary things! Redefining how leaders truly make a difference every single day by living the 5 Is can also be compared to living by the **virtues** defined by Lao Tzu, ancient Chinese philosopher and writer: living significantly, with kindness, support and reverence for all (242).

Staying Human

In our global and digitalized world with constant disruptive change, cultural differences and dealing with individuals with differing needs and interests, leaders are faced with immense challenges daily. To reflect this outside world, we expect leaders to adapt and be relevant at all times. This means leaders need to be stable yet flexible, coherent yet embracing complexity. If we also add the desire for a more connected and value-driven approach, this tight rope or balancing act will require mental and emotional stability.

First and foremost, **emotional intelligence** is key. As discussed in several earlier chapters, emotional intelligence is vital for connecting with self and others. High emotional intelligence is also a success factor in dealing with stressful situations as those with high emotional intelligence retain the ability for rational thinking and effective decision making even under pressure (75, 76).

Secondly, as leaders are often looked upon for guidance as well as support, and themselves receive diminishing feedback or support, it is essential that leaders draw their **confidence and energy** from elsewhere.

Thirdly, maintaining personal balance and emotional control to avoid the loss of ability to steer decisions and lead people can also be likened to staying sane (62), as **sanity** means the ability to think and behave in a normal and rational manner, with sound thinking and consistent behaviour at all times. There are four elements that summarize what must be in place for such stability:

1. Self-awareness and self-reflection – the need for self-assuredness in ourselves, understanding what we value, how we feel, what we think, how we behave and how we affect others.
2. Positive persona – relates to the ongoing need for a positive "brand" image and identity based on authenticity and optimism. All of which leaders need to be able to express to others.
3. Learning – Brain fitness is essential for mental and emotional development and this is achieved through new learning and augmenting ongoing skill and personal development.
4. Networking and relationships with others are vital as people need people. Leaders must strive to engage and support others, yet more importantly, must also have their own networks for support, outside of the team.

So, ask yourself, how do you remain human? How do you work on your emotional intelligence, where do you gain your confidence from and do you have all four elements in place to stay sane?

Stress Management

Choosing to be a leader must be driven by intrinsic care for other people. This is not about being popular or nice. For example, leaders with highly developed emotional intelligence can be tough by knowing exactly how far and how hard they can drive their people. Emotional intelligence can allow them to influence and bring people with them, even in difficult times when others naturally don't want to move (75, 76). Emotional intelligence also boosts performance because empathy is positively related to job performance and considerate managers have healthier staff. Emotionally available leaders are also less prone to experiencing workplace stress and can help other individuals become more reflective and better able to handle complex situations (78). However, what about when leaders experience stress themselves?

Stress is our body's natural short-term reaction to a situation or threat. It is a defensive mechanism, known as the "fight/flight response" and can include increased release of stress hormones such as adrenaline and cortisol, increased heart rate, reduced digestion and reduced immune responses. This is because the body is preparing itself. Historically, and evolutionary, the threat was physical attack yet today, stressors are more likely to be mental, emotional or social. It can result in feeling like losing control, anxiousness or being scared.

Like so much in management and leadership, stress is a balancing act!

Good effects	Bad effects
+ Focus	– Feels overwhelming
+ Alertness	– Keeps going
+ Increased performance	– Reduced performance

Figure 70: The Positive and Negative Effects of Stress

To understand stress, cope with it and build resistance, it is important to consider three elements (243):

Stressors – What is the threat or pressure, real or perceived? The problem.

Intensifiers – What internal issues are making it worse? Personal attitudes, beliefs (created or inherited), experiences or motives can reinforce the stressor and intensify the problem. Especially motives can make us over do it or show dysfunctional behaviours. Examples include desire to be perfect, be strong, hurry up, please others or try hard.

Reactions – Stress reactions include the physical body changes, emotions, thoughts and behaviours. If we experience stress it is important to gain awareness of all aspects of these reactions.

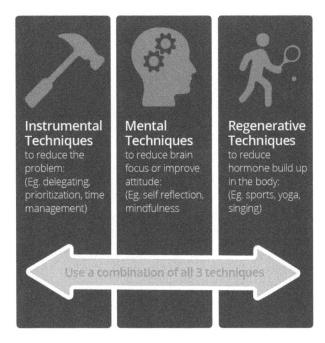

Figure 71: The Three Elements of Stress Management

The ability to cope with stress is based on cognitive appraisal of the belief we have in our resources to respond to the challenge of a stressor or change (244). Coping resources must match each of the 3 elements as managing stress requires effort on all 3 elements!

* Instrumental techniques to reduce the stressor
* Mental techniques to reduce the intensifiers
* Regenerative techniques to reduce the reactions

As a leader, stress is likely to be inevitable at times. What is important is knowing how to keep it a short-term reaction and how to avoid adding pressure unduly on others. It's about responsible behaviours towards others and overall organizational wellbeing.

Figure 72: Understanding Stress Versus Mental Health Issues

Though our personal ability to regulate our emotional response to stress varies (246), leaders can and should consider how to build **resilience** for personal stability (245). Resilience has much in common with many of the concepts we have already considered for effective transformational leadership driven by values. This circle of strong self and connectedness with others continues. Resilience is also built upon acceptance (letting go), optimism (mind set), future focus (vision), solution focus (goals), strong relationships/networks (connectedness), self-responsibility (accountability) and finally self-regulation to abandon the victim role (stuff happens so we have to learn from it). It all comes back to a solid, non-ego driven foundation for "self" that enables leaders to connect with and show kindness to others, at all times and especially when it matters most.

Key Learning Points

- Organizations driven by shared purpose will be best placed for sustainability despite many global challenges in the 21st century
- A transformational environment is one of focus, fulfilment and trust and comes from doing the right things for the organization (management) and doing them in the right way (leadership)
- The digital or virtual world does not have to be impersonal when driven by connectedness
- Leaders will be individuals who make a difference by having the courage to step forward, the curiosity to seek new ways and show kindness towards others
- Successful leaders will also demonstrate inner balance and resilience, the capacity to recover quickly from difficulties and keep learning and keep growing

Personal Reflection Points

Question 1: What does transformational leadership in the digital age mean to you?

	Examples of how you demonstrate each point in teams or projects	How do you believe you could be even better?
• Idealized influence	•	•
• Inspirational motivation	•	•
• Individualized consideration	•	•
• Intellectual stimulation	•	•
• Integrative support	•	•

Figure 73: Reflection Exercise on the 5 Is

Question 2:   How strong is your resilience?

	What can you strengthen?
• *Acceptance (letting go)*	•
• *Optimism (mind set)*	•
• *Future focus (vision)*	•
• *Solution focus (goals),*	•
• *Strong relationships/ networks (connectedness)*	•
• *Self-responsibility (accountability)*	•
• *Self-regulation to abandon the victim role*	•

Figure 74: **Reflection Exercise on Resilience**

Question 3:   What drives you? What personal change would you like to see?

Chapter 14

Tools to Transfer to Daily Work

In this chapter we summarize our key concepts and models so they are easy to find, easy to review and available to be transferred to your daily work.

The Role of Leaders

A leader is responsible and must therefore be accountable for the results of their team, project or area. The best leaders achieve results through people by balancing high focus on tasks with high focus on people (18). Too much focus on tasks may seem like transactional leadership and can work for short term delivery, however when sustained it feels like working for Rambo. Focus only on people whilst ignoring tasks and results breeds mediocrity. It may appear fun, but as people realize they are not succeeding, they will choose to leave.

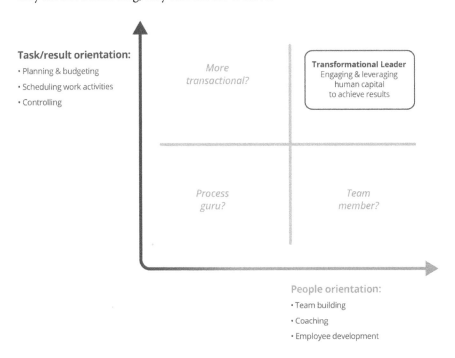

Figure 75: Representation of the Leadership Grid

Characteristics of Highly Successful Leaders

Leadership requires a combination of understanding who you are, how you act, how open you are, how available you are to others, as well as abilities to adapt to people and situations:

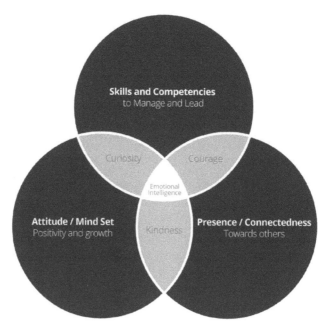

Figure 76: Characteristics of Successful Leaders

Management and Leadership Competencies

Competencies are transferable abilities which enable success in complex and unknown situations (56, 57). Competencies can be developed and strengthened and are important to understand as they have been shown to contribute more than intelligence in determining success. They indicate who is more likely to do a job better, even when skills and knowledge levels may be the same. Competencies can be selected for, used as qualitative performance measures during appraisals, and developed.

	Management	Leadership
Competencies	• Accountability • Planning & problem solving • Decision making • Strategic thinking & acting • Change management **Plus for people managers:** *Performance management* *Employee development*	• Idealized influence • Inspirational motivation • Individualized consideration • Intellectual stimulation • Integrative support
Meta-competencies	• Effective communication • Continuous learning	

Figure 77: Examples of Management and Leadership Competencies

For each of these "must have" management & meta-competencies, definitions and behavioural anchors are described below:

Accountability – A core competency, also linked to identification of future potential. This sense of ownership for self, others and results involves utilization of resources, decision making and actions within the scope of defined responsibilities. It can be described by:

• Acts independently within own area
• Is reliable in completing expected tasks or projects and is actively involved
• Ensures a smooth workflow at interfaces of work areas through communication, facilitation and integration of others – is willing to take over the lead or facilitate in group meetings and drives the group to results when required; can be a team player when required; sticks to agreed group actions/decisions
• Understands the responsibility for results
• Sees responsibility as a manager to support the team
• Shows high level of commitment towards the organization
• Bears consequences for personal actions, decisions and outcomes. Listens and accepts feedback accordingly.

Planning and problem solving – Cognitive abilities can be demonstrated through planning, problem solving, setting appropriate priorities and focus. As such, the competency refers to establishing a systematic course of action to ensure accomplishment of work, from analysing challenges through to generating solutions.

• Shows strong cognitive abilities to quickly identify key issues in complex scenarios; understands complexity and focuses on most relevant aspects and is able to identify interrelations between topics (lateral thinking)

- Able to balance a big picture perspective and the appropriate amount of details; shows a fact driven approach to planning and problem solving
- Collects information and data relevant to solve problems effectively, includes own and/or others' inputs as necessary
- Follows a structured work approach and keeps an overview on work tasks and progress; plans work with a realistic sense of the timeframe required
- Recognizes potential obstacles or difficulties and develops appropriate solutions; considers options and alternatives in the problem-solving process and does not jump to first or simplest conclusions
- Develops actionable plans with strong focus on implementation

Decision making – The cognitive process resulting in the selection of a course of action among several alternative possibilities. It is therefore the process of identifying and choosing alternatives based on knowledges, skills, experience, but also on the values, preferences and beliefs of the decision-maker. As a competency it can be described as:

- Willing and able to make decisions within own area of responsibility and able to do so on their own when necessary
- Making decisions in alignment with responsibilities and competencies and in a timely manner and based on information available
- Integrating knowledge and perspectives from others and in group settings actively involves others in the decision-making process, seeks inputs, integrates ideas from others; welcomes diverse perspectives
- Considering options, alternatives and consequences before making a decision
- Making decisions transparent to stakeholders, explaining reasons "why"
- Re-evaluating and correcting when necessary

Strategic thinking and acting – Alongside decision making, this is a key entrepreneurial competency required by senior leaders and project managers to shape direction. It ensures that actions are in alignment with organizational vision and predefined strategies and deals with the development of the organization and their area of responsibility. Abilities include:

- Understanding strategic concepts and how to align to daily work
- Relating to the organization's vision and business strategy when taking actions for own scope of responsibility; ensuring all contributions are in line with overall strategy and links corporate goals to team goals. Can communicate the organization's "story" succinctly and inspirationally
- Shows the ability to think holistically; considers the impact and consequences suggested actions might have on other parts of the organization (seeing inter-relations)

- Identifies relevant stakeholders, analyses their interests and undertakes actions accordingly
- Thinks broadly across departments when considering an overall strategic approach; uses an outside-in perspective when defining concepts and plans on a strategic level
- Future orientation: reflects on trends and innovative approaches to strategically explore future opportunities, sees where developments will lead and how they may influence the organization. Clearly understands the role as a leader to strategically think beyond the current status

Change management – A critical competency for innovation, sustaining competitive advantage and agile organizational development. It includes demonstrating support for continuous change to improve the organization's effectiveness and leading teams through the change process, helping others to overcome fears and resistance to refocus quickly back onto performance.

- Recognizes need for change and initiates measures and plans accordingly as a change driver or shaper
- Has a positive approach to change and is a role model in the change process
- Explains the necessity of change and helps employees to develop a clear understanding of what is expected as a result of the changes in the organization
- Understands project or task elements and the people elements in change (emotions and fears); can lead change by anticipating, strategizing, enabling and communicating to bring people through change
- Gains commitment and trust through new vision, effective stakeholder dialogue, inclusive projects and revised procedures/processes to ensure change is embedded
- Actively seeking improvements and ongoing changes in own area; facilitates and empowers team to make improvements

Performance management – is a key task of a manager and measures individual goal achievement and demonstration of organizational competencies, such as in annual appraisal meetings. The aim is to ensure delivery of tasks to meet company objectives. This includes conveying confidence in employees' abilities, sharing significant responsibility and authority and ensuring the assignment of tasks considering organization and department goals:

- Sets clear goals (SMART goals), assigns responsibilities and tasks according to abilities of the individual, keeps track of work results. Rewards completion and over achievement of goals. Manages under-achievement when required in a constructive manner.
- Ensures individual goals add up to team and departmental goal achievement.
- Provides the necessary resources for job completion, including skill-based training

• Grants employees decision rights within their own area of responsibility and supports self-dependent action; encourages and supports employees to make suggestions for improvement or to address new ideas openly

Employee development – A people-manager competency to develop team members' skills by planning effective actions related to current and future tasks and considering individual motivations and interests. Employee development however should be framed in the context of organizational vision, strategy and goals yet delivered individually to motivate, retain, nurture and grow, to maximise performance and develop potential talents for more expansive or senior roles. To achieve this, leaders require:

• Awareness of employees' strengths and individual development areas
• Discusses and prepares realistic development plans and supports employees in reaching their goals, aligned with organizational needs
• Expresses confidence in others' abilities to be successful and provides appropriate work challenges and on-the-job or near-job development opportunities
• Shows care and compassion for employees; provides honest, constructive and balanced feedback (both positive and critical) regarding performance and behaviour on a regular basis
• Shows good understanding of role and responsibility as manager; applies diverse measures for learning, invests own time in coaching and can create long term team plans
• Engages well one-to-one with employees; listens, asks questions, engages in genuine dialogue

Effective communication – A meta-competency for success with others and critical because it is how we come across to others as observable behaviour. Communication style is linked with first impressions we give others and is a conscious behaviour based on how we choose to motivate and influence others, and as such impacts employee engagement. As a competency it includes abilities to:

• Think with clarity
• Express ideas, facts and information consistently
• Choose appropriate language a multitude of differing audience types will best understand
• Handle the rapid flows of information within the organization, and among customers, partners, and other stakeholders and influencers
• Handle discrepancies and conflicts in a constructive manner
• Skills to support such outcomes include listening, engaging others in dialogue, utilizing ideas from others, facilitating meetings, summarizing discussions, actively distributing clear information, presenting concepts and facts, and inspiring emotionally

- In one-to-one settings welcomes appropriately (handshake), can create a positive and respectful atmosphere, asks questions and listens actively, stays calm. Is able to show empathy (empathetic dialogue), build rapport and convey difficult messages with balance of positive and negative inputs so recipients are able to buy into the messages. Can lead genuine conversations with open questions and appreciation and not back down when challenged
- In group settings is willing to speak up and influence the group, is able to get a message across, is accepted by the group, listened to. Explains reasoning / thinking to get buy-in and checks others are with them. Gets involved and actively contributes throughout the entire work process in groups and seeks to engage / include all, including other quieter team members actively by asking their opinion, asks specific questions and follows up
- In formal presentations can communicate ideas and opinions in a clear and comprehensible way; clear structure, key messages and summary. Uses supportive body language, good voice modulation, comes across as authentic and credible. Considers audience (relevancy, appropriate level, language and detail). Demonstrates the ability to inspire, spread enthusiasm and create buy-in; uses examples, stories or images for impact. Powerpoint presentations have clear structure (agenda), follow a clear storyline, balance text versus graphical elements well

Continuous learning – A meta-competency for all workers and one associated with higher potential for success in new roles and a criterion for top talents. Curiosity is an underlying attribute in learning, meaning being inquisitive, wondering, ready to poke around and figure something out. This requires ability and willingness to grow and change, in other words, a growth mind set. Demonstration of continuous learning includes the following behaviours:

- Continuously looking for ways to enhance knowledge & skills
- Actively involved in learning activities and adapting behaviour from learnings quickly
- Seeking opportunities for development and invests in personal learning
- Facing criticism, learning from mistakes
- Active self-reflection and evaluates own strengths and development areas in a realistic way
- Using feedback to improve performance
- Applying newly acquired skills and knowledge in daily work

For the leadership competencies, our **extended transformational model**, a model to create an environment of trust, is summarized here with key behavioural anchors for each of the 5 Is:

Competency	Idealized Influence	Inspirational Motivation	Individualized consideration	Intellectual Stimulation	Integrative Support
Theme	Role modelling	Setting direction for others	People orientation	Challenging the status quo	Digital connectedness
Behavioural anchors	• Leading by influence, from strong self-awareness • Acting authentically • Connecting personal & corporate values • Creating context • Ethical behaviour	• Building a vision with others • Using common purpose & achievement as motivator • Leveraging goal orientation • Speaking to inspire in all contexts	• Choosing to care • Showing empathy & appreciation • Coaching others • Recognizing individual strengths & developing accordingly	• Establishing flexibility & agility in teams • Creating an inclusive environment for ideas and innovation • Leveraging diversity & contribution from all	• Building and maintaining long term relationships • Creating team spirit and collaborative teamwork • Personal and team-focused networking • Digital mind set
Philosophical links for fulfilment	*Courage to work with purpose and significance*	*Bringing enthusiasm and passion*	*Showing reverence and kindness*	*Expanding curiosity and growth*	*Supportiveness to include everyone*

Figure 78: Overview of Key Behavioural Anchors of the Extended Transformational Leadership Model

Embedding Transformational Leadership as a Principle

Many organizations have embraced transformational leadership and implemented the competencies as part of their framework for success. This means they hire for, assess, reward and develop such leadership abilities as part of executive development programs. If you are looking to take such an approach, firstly consider if the organization's vision and values fit with these concepts or if this will be part of an overall transformational change? Change needs to be well planned and aligned to work, and include the following steps (138):

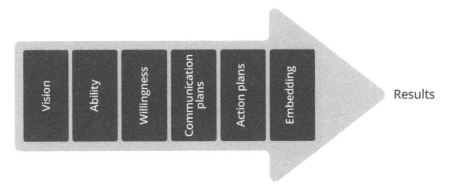

Figure 79: Steps for Leading Change

If any parts are missing from any change approach, this will negatively impact the results. Lack of a vision brings confusion. If the organization has no ability to deliver the change, there will be anxiety. Lack of willingness will mean no change at all. Without proper, well planned and well executed communication plans, resistance will wreak havoc and missing actions plans for the implementation details will cause many false starts. Finally, follow through and embedding new principles and behaviours, new systems etc for a competency framework, will be required for success, as without this, the goals of creating a transformational environment will not have been met.

'Progress is impossible without change, and those who cannot change their minds cannot change anything'

GEORGE BERNARD SHAW (118)

Bibliography and Notes

All of our concepts, and their application over many years, are based firmly in academic studies, however, our experiences of working in global companies, have also led us to adapt and develop much of the core theories we have shared here. This bibliography is intended to be as accurate as possible for original sources and the thinking of other experts. We do want to make it clear though that what we have found to work, and therefore used in this book, often blends multiple concepts and we apologise sincerely if, and when, we mis-quote or modify ideas beyond their original intention. Business and leadership are iterative, it is finding what works for you and what works in a given situation. If there was only one way, it would be easy! What we hope we have shown is that leadership for today and tomorrow can be different, can be based on meaning and connectedness and can be highly successful when leaders chose to act with courage, kindness and curiosity.

1. 21st Century Challenges is a programme of discussions and resources run by the Royal Geographical Society, to consider the biggest challenges in the coming decades. Their resources can be found at www.21stcenturychallenges.org
2. Kotter, John (2000). Kotter's Point of View: Leading in the 21st Century In HBR Working Knowledge archive. https://hbswk.hbs.edu/archive/kotter-s-point-of-view-leading-in-the-21st-century-0
3. Dalia Lama (2013). Dalai Lama's challenge: A 21st century of peace and compassion. A speech to Emory University. https://news.emory.edu/stories/2013/10/er_dalai_lama_talk_at_gwinnett/index.html
4. Dr Wayne W. Dyer was an internationally renowned author and speaker in the field of self-development. His latter works emphasised living with purpose and happiness, including The Shift: Taking Your Life From Ambition to Meaning (2010). Hay House Inc.
5. Rosen, Rob (2017). Lateral Leadership: A New Approach to Leadership in Today's Evolving Corporate Environment. http://www.cmpartners.com/negotiators-pause/lateral-leadership-new-approach-leadership-todays-evolving-corporate-environment/
6. Gallup Engagement Index (2019). www.gallup.de
7. The HR Research Institute (2019). The State of Employee Engagement in 2019: Leverage leadership and culture to maximize engagement. www.hr.com
8. Bartlett, Christopher A. & Ghoshal, Sumantra (1994). Beyond Strategy to Purpose. Harvard Business Review. Nov-Dec 1994 issue.
9. Porter, Michael E. (2001). The Value Chain and Competitive Advantage. In Understanding Business Processes, 50-66. Edited by David Barnes. Published by Psychology Press.
10. Drucker, Peter F. (1994). The Theory of the Business. Harvard Business Review. September–October 1994.
11. Fredmund Malik is an Austrian economist with focus on holistic management. His management tools, such as "The Wheel of Effectiveness", are valuable to understand management

tasks, and are published in many articles including MALIK, F. (2006). Führen Leisten Leben – Wirksames Management für eine neue Zeit. Frankfurt/Main: Campus Verlag GmbH.

12. Schein, Edgar. H. (1984). Coming to a New Awareness of Organizational Culture. Sloan Management Review, 25:2, p.3.

13. Northouse, Peter, G. (2013): Leadership: Theory and Practice. 6th ed. Thousand Oaks, CA: Sage Publications.

14. Malik, Fredmund. (2015). Managing Performing Living: Effective Management for a New Era. Frankfurt/New York: Campus.

15. Sahar Hashemi, Founder of Coffee Republic and author of several books including Switched On (2010). Published by Capstone.

16. Robison, Jennifer (2008). Turning Around Employee Turnover. From Gallup https://news. gallup.com/businessjournal/106912/turning-around-your-turnover-problem.aspx

17. Nink, Marco (2018). Engagement Index. Die neuesten Daten und Ergebnisse der Gallup-Studie. Munich: Redline Verlag.

18. Blake, R; Mouton, J; Bidwell, A. (1962): Managerial grid. In: Advanced Management – Office Executive, Vol 1(9), 1962, 12-15.

19. Hopper, Grace (1987) "The Wit and Wisdom of Grace Hopper". The OCLC Newsletter, No. 167, March/April 1987, from http://www.cs.yale.edu/homes/tap/Files/hopper-wit.html

20. Kotter, John (1990a). What Leaders Really Do. U.S.: Harvard Business Review Book. Kotter, John (1990b). What Leaders Really Do. Harvard Business Review, 68(3): May/June 1990.

21. Zaleznik, Abraham (1977/2004). Managers and Leaders: Are They Different? Harvard Business Review. January 2004 issue.

22. Psychology Today (2019), Bystander effect. From Psychologytoday.com/basics/bystander-effect. The Kitty Genovese murder case (1964) is also reviewed in the book: Bjergegaard, M. & Popa, C. (2016). How To Be A Leader. Pan Macmillan.

23. McClelland, David. (1961). The Achieving Society. Van Nostrand, Princeton.

24. Niklas Luhmann was a prominent German sociologist who published many works on power, trust, communication and organizational theory. Several of his books have been translated into English.

25. French, J. R. P. & Raven, B. (1959). The Bases of Social Power. In D. Cartwright and A. Zander. Group dynamics. New York: Harper & Row.

26. Horney, Nick et el. (2010). Leadership Agility: A Business Imperative for a VUCA World. People & Strategy. Vol 33/issue 4. http://luxorgroup.fr/coaching/wp-content/uploads/Leadership-agility-model.pdf.

27. John Francis "Jack" Welch, chairman and CEO of General Electric between 1981 and 2001, has published many books on change, competitive advantage and winning.

28. Kotter, John (2005). Leading Change – Why Transformation Efforts Fail. Harvard Business Review. Reprinted from: Kotter, J. (1995): Leading Change – Why transformation efforts fail. In: Harvard Business Review, March-April 1995.

29. Prof. Dr. Katrin Winkler has previously published work on changes in the digital age and extended transformational leadership. Though we summarize key aspects here, the full work can be seen in: Winkler, Katrin; Heinz, Tabea; Wagner, Barbara. (2020) Gut zu wissen: Herausforderung New Work – Wissen managen und Lernen fördern. In: Wörwag S., Cloots A. (eds) Zukunft der Arbeit – Perspektive Mensch. Springer Gabler, Wiesbaden.

30. Cisco (2016). 10th Annual Cisco Visual Networking Index (VNI) Mobile Forecast Projects 70 Percent of Global Population Will Be Mobile Users. https://newsroom.cisco.com/press-release-content?articleId=1741352

31. Elstner, S.; Feld, L. P.; Schmidt, C. M. (2016). Bedingtabwehrbereit: Deutschland im digitalen Wandel, Arbeitspapier, Sachverständigenrat zur Begutachtung der Gesamtwirtschaftlichen Entwicklung, No. 03/2016, Sachverständigenrat zur Begutachtung der Gesamtwirtschaftlichen Entwicklung, Wiesbaden.

32. Bundesministerium für Arbeit und Soziales (2017). Weissbuch Arbeiten 4.0. Berlin: Publikationsversand der Bundesregierung.

33. Hirsch-Kreinsen, H. (2015). Einleitung: Digitalisierung industrieller Arbeit. In: Hirsch-Kreinsen, H., Ittermann, P., Niehaus, J. Digitalisierung industrieller Arbeit. Die Vision Industrie 4.0 und ihre sozialen Herausforderungen. Baden-Baden: Nomos Verlagsgesellschaft

34. Experton Group AG (2015). Digitale Transformation – Status Quo. http://research. isg-one.de/fileadmin/experton/consulting/digital/Experton_Group_WP__Digitale_ Transformatio_Status_quo.pdf

35. Bruch, H. & Berenbold, S. (2017). Zurück zum Kern. Sinnstiftende Führung in der Arbeitswelt 4.0 In: Organisationsentwicklung 1/2017.

36. Jäger, W. & Körner, P. (2016). New Work, New Leadership. In: Petry. T. Digital Leadership – Erfolgreiches Führen in Zeiten der Digital Economy, S.99-114. Freiburg: Haufe-Lexware GmbH & Co. KG.

37. Flecker, J.; Riesenecker-Caba, T.; Schönauer, A. (2016). Sozialbericht 2015-2016: Arbeit 4.0 – Auswirkungen technologischer Veränderungen auf die Arbeitswelt. Wien: Bundesministerium für Arbeit, Soziales, Gesundheit und Konsumentenschutz.

38. Schermuly, C. C. (2016). New Work – gute Arbeit gestalten: psychologisches Empowerment von Mitarbeitern. Freiburg: Haufe Gruppe.

39. Schmidt, T. (2018). Performance Management im Wandel – Sollten Unternehmen ihre Mitarbeiterbeurteilungen abschaffen? Wiesbaden: Springer Gabler.

40. Bauer, W. (2015). Smarter Working – Menschen. Räume. Technologien. Die digitale Transformation von Gesellschaft und Wirtschaft. Wirtschaftspolitische Blätter 1/2015.

41. Kratzer, N.; Menz, W.; Pangert, B. (2015). Work-Life-Balance – eine Frage der Leistungspolitik. *Analysen und Gestaltungsansätze*. Wiesbaden: Springer VS.

42. Brenke, K. (2016). Home Office: Möglichkeiten werden bei weitem nicht ausgeschöpft. In: DIW-Wochenbericht, Jg. 83, 5/2016.

43. Schwarzmüller, T.; Brosi, P.; Welpe, I. M. (2017). Führung 4.0 – Wie die Digitalisierung Führung verändert, In: Hildebrandt, Alexandra; Landhäußer, Werner (2017). CSR und Digitalisierung – Der digitale Wandel als Chance und Herausforderung für Wirtschaft und Gesellschaft. Berlin: Springer-Gabler.

44. Bruch, H. & Berenbold, S. (2017). Zurück zum Kern. Sinnstiftende Führung in der Arbeitswelt 4.0. Organisationsentwicklung 1/2017.

45. Burns, James M. (1978). Leadership. New York: Harper & Row.

46. Bass, Bernard M. (1990). Bass & Stogdill's Handbook of Leadership: Theory, Research and Managerial Applications, 3. Aufl. New York et al.

47. Hamel, Gary. (2007). The Future of Management. Harvard Business School Press.

48. O'Reilly, C.A., *et al.* (2010). How Leadership Matters: The effects of leaders' alignment on strategy implementation. The Leadership Quarterly, 2010 issue 21. https://faculty.haas. berkeley.edu/CHATMAN/papers/04_HowLeadershipMatters.pdf

49. Sutevski (2018). Effects of Good Leadership on Employees. From https://www. entrepreneurshipinabox.com/13305/6-effects-good-leadership-employees

50. Liebermeister, Barbara. (2017). Digital ist egal: Mensch bleibt Mensch – Führung entscheidet. Offenbach: GABAL Verlag.

51. Creusen, U.; Gall, B.; Hackl, O. (2017). Digital Leadership – Führung in Zeiten des digitalen Wandels. Wiesbaden: Springer Fachmedien Wiesbaden GmbH.

52. IFIDZ (Institut für Führung im digitalen Zeitalter) (2016). Führen im digitalen Zeitalter –Relevante Kompetenzen und Anforderungen an Führungskräfte.

53. Bass, Bernard M. (1985): Leadership and Performance beyond expectations. New York: Free Press.

54. Cherry, K. (2018). The Great Man Theory of Leadership. From Verywellmind, updated Nov 242018. https://www.verywellmind.com/the-great-man-theory-of-leadership-2795311

55. Isaacson, Walter. (2011). Steve Jobs. Simon & Schuster, New York. Isaacson, Walter. (2012). The Real Leadership Lessons of Steve Jobs. From April 2012 issue Harvard Business Review.

56. Erpenbeck, J.; Von Rosenstiel, L. (2003). Handbuch Kompetenzmessung. Stuttgart: Schäffer-Poeschel.

57. Tubbs, S. L., & Schulz, E. (2006). Exploring a Taxonomy of Global Leadership Competencies and Meta-Competencies. Journal of American Academy of Business, Cambridge, 8(2).

58. In 2017, Emma Walmsley was appointed new CEO of GSK, the first woman to head up a major global pharmaceutical company. In 2018 she was awarded Britain's Most Admired Leader by journal Management Today. Before GSK she was General Manager for Garnier/ Maybelline at L'Oréal. Her success as a world-class leader is attributed to a winning combination of IQ, technical experience from a variety of international marketing and management roles, commercial savviness and EQ, enabling her to engage and motivate others to be the very best that they can be. Source: Cannon, Kate (2019). https://diademperformance.com/secret-emma-walmsleys-leadership-success/. In interviews, Walmlsey openly discusses her leadership style and success. Source: https://www.youtube.com/watch?v=PPa5DevzAK0

59. Dweck, Carol. (2007). Mindset: The New Psychology of Success. New York: Ballantine Books.

60. Abigail Adams was First Lady of USA as wife of President John Adams, 1797-1801. She was his most trusted advisor and avid letter writer.

61. Eichlinger, Bob & Lombardo, Mike (1996). Coined the 70/20/10 formula from CCL research. Source: CENTER FOR CREATIVE LEADERSHIP (n.d.): The 70-20-10 Rule for Leadership Development. https://www.ccl.org/articles/leading-effectively-articles/70-20-10-rule/

62. Perry, Philippa. (2012). How To Stay Sane. MacMillan Publishers Ltd. A truly inspiring book on the psychology of who we are and how to enhance welling being and relationships.

63. Fisk, P. (2017). Education 4.0 … the future of learning will be dramatically different, in school and throughout life. https://www.thegeniusworks.com/2017/01/future-education-young-everyone-taught-together/

64. Podsakoff, P. M.; MacKenzie, S. B.; Bommer, W. H. (1996). Transformational leader behaviors and substitutes for leadership as determinants of employee satisfaction, commitment, trust and organizational citizenship behaviors. Journal of Management, 22.

65. Felfe, J. (2005). Charisma, transformationale Führung und Commitment. Köln: Kölner Studien Verlag.

66. Wang, Y.; Zheng, Y. (2018). How transformational leadership influences employee voice behaviour: The roles of psychological capital and organizational identification. In Social Behavior and Personality, 2018, 46(2).

67. Bass, B. M.; Riggio, R. E. (2006). Transformational Leadership, 2. Aufl., London: Mahwah.

68. Avolio, B. J.; Bass, B. M. (1991). The Full Range Leadership Development. Binghamton: Bass, Avolio and Associates.

69. Kearney, E.; Gebert, D. (2009). Managing Diversity and Enhancing Team Outcomes: The Promise of Transformational Leadership. Journal of Applied Psychology, 94, 2009.

70. Kark, R., & Shamir, B. (2002). The Influence of Transformational Leadership on Followers' Relational versus Collective Self-Concept. Academy of Management Annual Meeting Proceedings, No. 1, D1-D6, 2002.

71. Kark, R., Shamir, B. and Chen, G. (2003). The Two Faces of Transformational Leadership: Empowerment and Dependency. Journal of Applied Psychology, 88, 2003.

72. Hoyt, C.L. & Blascovich, J. (2003). Transformational and transactional leadership in virtual and physical environments, in: SMALL GROUP RESEARCH, Vol. 34 No. 6, December 2003.

73. Bass, B. M. & Avolio, B. J. (1990). The Implications of Transactional and Transformational Leadership for Individual, Team, and Organizational Development, in: Pasmore, W. A./ Woodman, R.W. Research in Organizational Change and Development: An Annual Series Featuring Advances in Theory, Methodology and Research, Vol. 4., Greenwich.

74. When referring to self-awareness, Chartered Management Institute (2018) claimed that "85% of people do not have this essential skill".

75. Goleman, Daniel. (1995). Emotional Intelligence: Why It Can Matter More than IQ. New York: Bantam Books.

76. Goleman, Daniel. (2000). Leadership That Gets Results. Harvard Business Review, 78 (2), 2000.

77. Judge, T.A., et al. (2002). Personality and Leadership: A qualitative and quantitative review. Journal of Applied Psychology, 87, 2002.

78. Haughton, J. (2018). Five reasons we need to show emotion in the boardroom. 18 January 2018. https://www.managers.org.uk/insights/news/2018/january/five-reasons-we-need-to-show-emotion-in-the-boardroom

79. Brousseau, K. & Driver, M. (2004). Career View: Roadmaps for Career Success. Decision Dynamics LLC.

80. Hays Group Report (2016). Women Outperform Men in 11 of 12 Key Emotional Intelligence Competencies. Hay Group division of Korn Ferry. https://www.kornferry.com/press/new-research-shows-women-are-better-at-using-soft-skills-crucial-for-effective-leadership.

81. Brousseau, K., Driver, M., Hourihan, G. & Larsson, R. (2011). The Seasoned Executive's Decision-Making Style. Harvard Business Review, Feb. 2011.

82. Probst, G. & Eppler, M. J. (1998). Persönliches Wissensmanagement in der Unternehmensführung. Zeitschrift für Organisation und Führung, 3.

83. Leadership Insight Assessment® from Decision Dynamics LLC. Source: https://www.mydecisionstyle.com/

84. Grossman, David (2017). How Much Time Do You Spend Communicating? https://www.yourthoughtpartner.com/blog/how-much-time-do-you-spend-communicating

85. Crawford, C.B. & Strohkirch, C.S. (2006). The Critical Role of Communication In Knowledge Organizations: Communication Apprehension As A Predictor Of Knowledge Management Functions. Journal of Knowledge Management Practice, Vol. 7, No. 4, December 2006.

86. Five Modes of Communication are key for relating to others. They link to Martin Buber's descriptions of communication types from technical dialogue to genuine dialogue. Source: Perry, Philippa. (2012) How To Stay Sane. MacMillan Publishers Ltd.

87. McGee, Paul. (2013). How to Succeed With People. Capstone Publishing. McGee is one of the best writers for showing how to use emotional intelligence to engage, influence and motivate people, in a fun and simple way. A highly recommended read!

88. DISC has its origins from Carl Gustav Jung, 1921, where he described psychological types. In 1928, William Moulton Marston then published "The Emotions of Normal People" which describes the DISC theory used today. DISC assessments and tools are available from several commercial sources.

89. Kuhl, S. & Matthiesen, K. (2012). Wenn man mit Hierarchie nicht weiterkommt: Zur Weiterentwicklung des Konzepts des Lateralen Führens. In: Die Zukunft der Führung. Grote S (Ed); Heidelberg: Springer Gabler.

90. Johnson, L. (2003): Exerting Influence Without Authority. Harvard Management Update, Dec 2003.

91. Bittelmeyer, A. (2007). Managen ohne Weisungsbefugnis. Laterale Führung. managerSeminare, Heft 108.

92. Rousseau, D. *et al.* (1998): Not so different after all: A cross-discipline view of trust. In: Academy of Management Review, 23, 1998.

93. Peter Drucker, quoted in Cummings, K. (2013). Trust, Communication, and Leadership: The Three Laws of Influence. http://www.astd.org/Publications/Blogs/Management-Blog/2013/04/Trust-Communication-and-Leadership-the-Three-Laws-of-Influence

94. Watzlawick, P. (1967). Pragmatics of Human Communication: A Study of International Patterns, Pathologies, and Paradoxes. W. W. Norton & Company.

95. Zeffane, R.; Tipu, S.; Ryan, J. (2011). Communication, Commitment & Trust: Exploring the Triad. In: International Journal of Business and Management, Vol. 6, Nr. 6, June 2011.

96. UK Government MacLeod Review. Sept 2009. Engaging For Success.

97. Cialdini, R.B. (2006). Influence: The Psychology of Persuasion, Revised Edition Revised Edition 2006.

98. Cialdini, R.B. (2012). Influence At Work. http://www.influenceatwork.com. Published on Nov 26, 2012. https://www.youtube.com/watch?v=cFdCzN7RYbw.

99. McGregor, Douglas (1960). The Human Side of Enterprise. New York, McGraw-Hill Books Company Inc.

100. Pitts, A. (2013). You Only Have 7 Seconds To Make A Strong First Impression. Apr. 8, 2013. https://www.businessinsider.com/only-7-seconds-to-make-first-impression-2013-4?r=US&IR=T

101. Ebersole, G. (2015). Dress for success: The importance of your workplace attire. March 2, 2015. https://www.readingeagle.com/business-weekly/article/dress-for-success-the-importance-of-your-workplace-attire

102. Robertson Davies, Canadian author (1913-1995).

103. Perry, Grayson (2017). The Descent of Man. Penguin Random House UK.

104. McCafferty, N. (2009). How not to dress for a job in the recession. PUBLISHED July 27, 2009. https://www.express.co.uk/news/weird/116732/How-not-to-dress-for-a-job-in-the-recession

105. How Much Can You Trust Your Brain? (2018). How It Works, Issue 118.

106. Hunt, V.; Layton, D.; Prince, S. (2015). Diversity Matters. McKinsey & Company. https://www.mckinsey.com/~/media/mckinsey/business%20functions/organization/our%20insights/why%20diversity%20matters/diversity%20matters.ashx

107. Zayas, V. (2016). Impressions Based on a Portrait Predict, 1-Month Later, Impressions Following a Live Interaction. Social Psychological and Personality Science 2016 and quoted in https://www.express.co.uk/news/uk/737712/first-impression-judgement-people-research 2016

108. Randall, Matthew (2010). Dress for Success. Source: https://prosperative.net/dress-for-success-the-importance-of-your-workplace-attire/

109. Campbell, Alistair (2015). Winners. And How They Succeed. Penguin Random House UK.

110. Peters, Tom (1997). The Brand Called You. August 31, 1997. Fast Company Magazine.

111. Hodgson, S. (2017). What is personal branding? Building your personal brand. May 25, 2017. http://fabrikbrands.com/what-is-personal-branding/

112. Sinek, Simon (2009). Start with Why: How Great Leaders Inspire Everyone to Take Action. Portfolio.

113. McCormack, Joseph (2014). BRIEF. Make a bigger impact by saying less. John Wiley & Sons.

114. Mehrabian, Albert (1971). Silent Messages. Wadsworth Publishing Company Inc.

115. Gruenfeld, Deborah. (2013). Power & Influence. Mar 13, 2013. https://www.youtube.com/watch?v=KdQHAeAnHmw

116. Souza, J. (2014) Mark Zuckerberg, gray T-shirts, and personal branding. November 11, 2014. http://www.socialmediaimpact.com/mark-zuckerberg-grey-t-shirts-art-personal-branding/

117. Bellezza, S. *et al* (2014). The Red Sneakers Effect: Inferring Status and Competence from Signals of Nonconformity. JOURNAL OF CONSUMER RESEARCH, Inc. Vol. 41, June 2014. Source: https://www.bbc.co.uk/news/technology-48472408

118. Shaw, George Bernard. Playwrite (1856-1950).

119. Winkler, Katrin & Saur, Christina (2019). Employee Retention Management: long-term retention of employees – a comparison of generations. Journal of Applied Leadership and Management, Journal of Applied Leadership and Management, 2019 Vol 7.

120. Research by Hogan *et al* 1994 and Yukl 1998, and quoted in: Judge, T.A., *et al.* (2002). Personality and leadership: A qualitative and quantitative review. Journal of Applied Psychology, 87, 2002.

121. George, Bill; Sims, Peter; McLean, Andrew N.; Mayer, Diana (2007). Discovering Your Authentic Leadership. Harvard Business Review. Issue 129 February 2007.

122. Kilroy J. Oldster, author (1902-1962).

123. Schuck, Heather (2013). The Working Mom Manifesto. Voyager Media, Inc.

124. Oprah Winfrey, media proprietor, talk show host, actress, producer, philanthropist. One of top 10 richest women in America, 1 of 7 self-made female billionaires.

125. McGee, Paul (2005). SUMO Shut Up, Move On. Capstone Publishing Ltd.

126. Price Waterhouse Coopers (2011). Millennials at work – Reshaping the workplace. https://www.pwc.de/de/prozessoptimierung/assets/millennials-at-work-2011.pdf

127. Best Companies Awards. https://www.b.co.uk/

128. Davidson, Hugh J. (2005). The Committed Enterprise: Making Vision, Values, and Branding Work. GB: Elsevier/Butterworth-Heinemann.

129. Thompson, C. (2018). Leadership behaviours that nurture organizational trust: Re-examining the fundamentals. Journal of Human Resource Management, vol. XXI, 1/2018.

130. Mayer, M *et al.* (2012). Who displays ethical leadership, and why does it matter? An examination of antecedents and consequences of ethical leadership. Academy of Management Journal 2012, Vol. 55, No. 1.

131. McLeod, D. & Clarke, N. (2009). Engaging for success: enhancing performance through employee engagement: a report to government. http://hdl.voced.edu.au/10707/149387

132. Tanner, C. *et al.* (2010). Actions Speak Louder Than Words. The Benefits of Ethical Behaviors of Leaders. Journal of Psychology 2010; Vol. 218(4).

133. Rawolle, M. & Kehr, H. (2012). Lust auf Zukunft – Die motivierende Kraft von Unternehmensvisionen verstehen und nutzen. Organisationsentwicklung 04/12.

134. Senator John F Kennedy (1960). Speech at The Coliseum, Raleigh, North Carolina. September 17, 1960. https://www.jfklibrary.org/archives/other-resources/john-f-kennedy-speeches/raleigh-nc-19600917

135. Davenport, T. H.; Harris; J. & Shapiro, J. (2010). Competing on talent analytics. Harvard Business Review, 10-2010.

136. Kotter, John (2012). Leading change. U.S.: Harvard Business Review Press.

137. Steve Brechter is a seasoned senior executive with expertise in leading organizations through transformation and change. https://www.graystoneadvisors.com/steve-brechter/

138. Lippert, M. (1987) as cited by CLI (Curriculum Leadership Institute). Managing Transformational Change Efforts. https://cliweb.org/wp-content/uploads/2016/01/TransformationalChange2-1.pdf

139. "We choose to go to the Moon", officially titled as the Address at Rice University on the Nation's Space Effort, is a speech delivered by United States President John F. Kennedy about the effort to reach the Moon at Rice Stadium in Houston, Texas, on September 12, 1962.

140. This quote is commonly attributed to Albert Einstein though no substantive evidence exists suggesting Einstein made this statement, yet we whole heartedly agree with its sentiment.

141. Quote from an interview with Astronaut Kathryn Sullivan. New Scientist. 18 January 2020.

142. Locke, E. A. *et al.* (1990) A Theory of Goal Setting & Task Performance. Prentice-Hall.

143. Pink, D. (2009). Drive. The surprising truth about what motivates us. New York: Riverhead Books

144. Herzberg, F. (1968/2003). One more time: How do you motivate employees? In: Harvard Business Review, January 2003 LOCKE, E. A.

145. Deci, E. L., & Ryan, R. M. (2000). The "what" and "why" of goal pursuits: Human needs and the self-determination of behavior. Psychological Inquiry, 11, 2000.

146. Deci, E. L., & Ryan, R. M. (2008). Self-Determination Theory: A macrotheory of human motivation, development, and health. Canadian Psychology/Psychologie Canadienne, 49, 2008.

147. Anne Morrow Lindbergh, author (1906-2001)

148. Ng, T. W. H. (2017). Transformational leadership and performance outcomes. The Leadership Quarterly, 28, 2017.

149. Murray, K. (2014). Communicate to Inspire – a guide for leaders. Kogan Page

150. James C Humes, US lawyer, author and former presidential speech writer.

151. Covey, Steven (1990). The Seven Habits of Highly Effective People. New York: Fireside Book

152. Kouzes, J. M. & Posner, B. Z. (2012). The Leadership Challenge: How to Make Extraordinary Things Happen in Organizations. Jossey-Bass Publishing.

153. Schartz, Tony (2012). Managing People. Why Appreciation Matters So Much. January 23, 2012.

154. Harvard Mental Health Publishing (Nov 2011) In Praise of Gratitude. Harvard Mental Health Letter. https://www.health.harvard.edu/newsletter_article/in-praise-of-gratitude

155. Roger Joseph Ebert was an American film critic, historian, journalist, screenwriter, and author (1942-2013).

156. Goleman, Daniel (2013). Empathy 101. 2013-10-13. http://www.danielgoleman.info/empathy-101/

157. Hays plc. (2014). HR Report 2014/2015: Schwerpunkt Führung. from https://www.hays.de/personaldienstleistung-aktuell/studie/hr-report-2014-2015-schwerpunkt-fuehrung

158. Whitmore, John (2009). Coaching for Performance: The Principles and Practices of Coaching and Leadership, 4th ed., Nicholas Brealey Publishing.

159. Grant, A. M. (2006). An Integrative Goal-Focused Approach to Executive Coaching. In D. R. Stober & A. M. Grant (Eds.), Evidence based coaching handbook: Putting best practices to work for your clients. Hoboken, NJ, US: John Wiley & Sons Inc.

160. Nicholson, N. (2013). The I of Leadership. Jossey-Bass Publishing

161. Landberg, M. (2015) The Tao of Coaching: Boost Your Effectiveness at Work by Inspiring and Developing Those Around You, updated ed., Profile Books.

162. Hersey, P., & Blanchard, K. H. (1969). Life cycle theory of leadership. Training & Development Journal, 23(5), 26, 1969.

163. Hersey, P., & Blanchard, K. H. (1996). Great ideas revisited: Revisiting the life-cycle theory of leadership. Training & Development Journal, 50(1), 42.

164. Clutterbuck, D. & Schneider, S. (1998). Executive mentoring, Croner's Executive Companion. Bulletin, Issue 29, October 1998.

165. www.forum-mentoring.de/index.php/mentoring_top/mentoring/begriffsklarung

166. Bellevue University's Human Capital Lab (2010). Case Study: Sun Microsystems University Mentoring.

167. Dryburgh, A. (2011). Everything You Know About Business is Wrong. Headline Publishing.

168. Steinweg, S. (2009). Systematisches Talent Management. S. 2. Stuttgart: Schäffer-Poeschel

169. Csíkszentmihályi, M. (1990) Flow: The Psychology of Optimal Experience. Harper Perennial Modern Classics.

170. Aguinis, Herman (2013). Performance Management. 3rd Edition. Pearson Education Inc, Prentice Hall.

171. Clifton, D. O. & Harter, J. K. (2014). Investing in strengths. https://www.researchgate. net/profile/James_Harter/publication/242468710_Investing_in_strengths/ links/53e39aed0cf25d674e91b306/Investing-in-strengths.pdf

172. Linley, A. (2008). Average to A+: Realising strengths in yourself and others. Coventry, UK: CAPP Press (2008), 9.

173. Page, Kathryn M. & Vella-Brodrick, Dianne A. (2009). The 'What', 'Why' and 'How' of Employee Well-Being: A New Model. Social Indicators Research. February 2009, Volume 90, Issue 3.

174. Krivkovich, A. *et al.* (2017). Women in the Workplace McKinsey Survey October 2017 Report, from https://www.mckinsey.com/featured-insights/gender-equality/women-in-the-workplace-2017

175. Stone, D. M. & Heen, S. (2014). Thanks for the Feedback: The Science and Art of Receiving Feedback Well. Viking.

176. Gunkel, L. & Mandl, H. (2013). Acceptance and Effects of Feedback in Individual Psychological Assessments. Paper presented on the 6th International Conference of Education (ICERI), November 18 to November 20, 2013, Sevilla, Spain

177. Heen, S. & Stone, D. M. (2014). Find the Coaching in Criticism. Harvard Business Review. January–February 2014 Issue.

178. McKinsey developed the 9 Box Matrix in the 1970s to help GE prioritize investments across its business units. It is a commonly used tool today for plotting team members' performance and potential.

179. Henry Kissinger, American politician, diplomat and author.

180. Beck, K. *et al.* (2001). Manifesto for Agile Software Development. http://agilemanifesto.org/

181. Schwaber, K. & Sutherland, J. (2017). The Scrum Guide™ – The Definitive Guide to Scrum: The Rules of the Game. https://www.scrumguides.org/docs/scrumguide/v2017/2017-Scrum-Guide-US.pdf#zoom=100

182. Brown, T. (2008). Design Thinking. Harvard Business Review. June 2008.

183. Janis, I. (1982). Groupthink. 2nd edition. Houghton Mifflin: Boston.

184. Lovegrove, H. (2010). Inspirational Leadership. Linchpin Books.

185. Higginbottom, K. (2018). Why The Ability To Fail Leads To Innovation. www.forbes.com/ sites/karenhigginbottom/2017/08/03/why-the-ability-to-fail-leads-to-innovation/

186. How Google made its teams more creative (2019). An edited extract from Make Elephants Fly: The Process of Radical Innovation by Steven S. Hoffman , CMI Management Book of the Year 2019. https://www.managers.org.uk/insights/news/2019/february/mboty-2019-how-google-made-its-teams-more-creative?utm_source=Chartered%20Management%20

Institute&utm_medium=email&utm_campaign=10335174_Insights%201%20March%20
2019&dm_i=SYT,65IO6,4K4NB8,O78X7,1

187. Lunney, J.; Lueder, S.; O´Connor, G. (2018). Postmortem culture: how you can learn from failure. https://rework.withgoogle.com/blog/postmortem-culture-how-you-can-learn-from-failure/

188. Spencer, J. (2017). Think inside the box. Published in: Educational Leadership, October 2017.

189. Dunbar, A. (2013). Solution to the 'Nine Dots' problem – thinking outside of the box. https://www.youtube.com/watch?v=JOvjIAbB2i8

190. Rigie, M. & Harmeyer, K. (2018). How to think outside the box. Smart Storming LLC. https://www.smartstorming.com/think-outside-box-video/

191. Kline, N. (2004). Thinking caps off. People Management. https://www.timetothink.com/uploaded/PM%20article.pdf

192. Granig, Peter & Hartlieb, Erich (2012). Die Kunst der Innovation. Springer Gabler.

193. Drucker, Peter F. (1985). Innovation and Entrepreneurship. Heinemann, London.

194. Vivek ,Siva (2018). https://www.hackerearth.com/blog/innovation-management/co-innovation-concept-benefits-examples/

195. https://eit.europa.eu/eit-innovation-hubs

196. Tim Berners-Lee, British physicist and inventor of the World Wide Web.

197. Hewlett, S.; Marshall, M.; Sherbin, L. (2013). How Diversity can drive Innovation. Harvard Business Review. December 2013.

198. Economist Intelligence Unit Survey, Oct 2013.

199. McKinsey (2016). Women in the Workplace Survey. 2016 Report from https://www.mckinsey.com/business-functions/organization/our-insights/women-in-the-workplace-2016

200. Levine, S. & Stark, D. (2015). Diversity Makes You Brighter, The New York Times, Dec 9th 2015.

201. Johnson, S.K. (2017). What 11 CEOs Have Learned About Championing Diversity. Harvard Business Review. August 29, 2017

202. Blanchard, K. (2011). https://leadingwithtrust.com/category/circles-of-trust/

203. Similarity Attraction. http://www.faz.net/aktuell/gesellschaft/menschen/menschen-mit-gemeinsamkeiten-ziehen-sich-an-13948519-p3.html

204. Kahnemann, Daniel (2012). Thinking, Fast and Slow. Penguin.

205. Krivkovich, A. et al. (2017). Women in the Workplace McKinsey Survey October 2017 Report, https://www.mckinsey.com/featured-insights/gender-equality/women-in-the-workplace-2017

206. Desvaux, G.; Devillard, S.; Sancier-Sultan, S. (2010). Woman Matter 2010. https://www.mckinsey.com/~/media/McKinsey/Business%20Functions/Organization/Our%20Insights/Women%20at%20the%20top%20of%20corporations%20Making%20it%20happen/Women%20at%20the%20top%20of%20corporations%20Making%20it%20happen.ashx

207. Neil Lenane, Talent Acquisition, Diversity and Inclusion Leader at Progressive Insurance.

208. Hoch, J. & Korlowski, S. (2014). Leading Virtual Teams: Hierarchical Leadership, Structural Support and Shared Team Leadership. Journal of Applied Psychology, vol 99, no 3.

209. Margaret Carty, author.

210. Mortensen, M. (2015). A First-Time Managers Guide to Leading Virtual Teams. Harvard Business Review, September 25, 2015.

211. Edinger, S. (2012). Why Remote Workers Are More (Yes, More) Engaged. Harvard Business Review. August 24, 2012.

212. Jarrett, C. (2015). How Facebook is Changing Our Social Lives. World Economic Forum, October 2015.

213. Ward, S. (2019). What Is Business Networking & What Are the Benefits? How to Make the Most of the Benefits of Business Networking. https://www.thebalancesmb.com/what-is-business-networking-and-what-are-the-benefits-2947183

214. Littlejohn, A.; Milligan, C.; Margaryan, A.(2011). Collective learning in the workplace: important knowledge sharing behaviours. International Journal of Advanced Corporate Learning, 4(4).

215. Ibarra H. & Hunter M. L. (2007). How Leaders Create and Use Networks. Harvard Business Review, January 2007.

216. Bennett, S. (2013). CEOs Using Social Media: Statistics, Facts And Figures. Adweek. https://www.adweek.com/digital/social-ceo-stats/

217. Dottie, C. (2017). 6 reasons leaders need to raise their social media game. Siliconrepublic. https://www.siliconrepublic.com/advice/leaders-social-media-tips-hays

218. Dunay, P. (2014). From Employee to Advocate: Mobilize Your Team to Share Your Brand Content. Social Media Today https://www.socialmediatoday.com/content/employee-advocate-mobilize-your-team-share-your-brand-content

219. Richard Branson, Founder of Virgin Group.

220. Aagaard, A. (2019). Digital Business Models. Palgrave Macmillan.

221. European Union (2012). Digital Competence in Practice: An Analysis of Framework.

222. European Union (2017). The Digital Competence Framework for Citizens.

223. Aaron Dignan, American businessman and author.

224. Nielsen, K. & Daniels, K. (2016). The relationship between transformational leadership and follower sickness absence: the role of presenteeism. Work & Stress, 2016; 1.

225. Czaja, J. (2018). The Trouble With Transformational Leadership. https://smallbusiness.chron.com/trouble-transformational-leadership-21793.html

226. Conley, R. (2018). Three Proven Strategies for Leading Virtual Teams on Leading with Trust. https://leadingwithtrust.com/2018/05/27/3-proven-strategies-for-leading-virtual-teams/

227. Catalyst.org (2019) Quick Take: Generations—Demographic Trends in Population and Workforce. Aug 20, 2018. https://www.catalyst.org/research/generations-demographic-trends-in-population-and-workforce/

228. Emmons, M. (2018). Key Statistics about Millennials in the Workplace. October 9, 2018. Dynamic Signals Inc. https://dynamicsignal.com/2018/10/09/key-statistics-millennials-in-the-workplace/

229. Sinek, Simon (2016). Millennials in the Workplace Interview https://ochen.com/transcript-of-simon-sineks-millennials-in-the-workplace-interview/

230. Andrews, W.& Cain, M. (2018). Millennial Digital Workers Really Do Differ From Their Elders. Published: 27 February 2018. https://www.gartner.com/doc/3862563/millennial-digital-workers-really-differ

231. Great Place To Work Institute (2018) Best Workplaces for Millennials Survey Summary. https://www.greatplacetowork.com/resources/reports/2018-best-workplaces-for-millennials-summary

232. Manpower Group (2016). Millennial Careers: 2020 Vision. https://www.manpowergroup.com/wps/wcm/connect/660ebf65-144c-489e-975c-9f838294c237/MillennialsPaper1_2020Vision_lo.pdf?MOD=AJPERES

233. Twenge, Jean M. (2017). iGen: Why Today's Super-Connected Kids Are Growing Up Less Rebellious, More Tolerant, Less Happy--and Completely Unprepared for Adulthood--and What That Means for the Rest of Us.; 2nd Print edition. Atria Books.

234. Peterson, M. (2004). What men and women value at work: Implications for workplace health. Gender Medicine. December 2004.

235. Center for Creative Leadership. (2019). What Women Want From Work. https://www.ccl.org/blog/what-women-want-work/February 24, 2019.

236. Nierenberg, S (2008). Catalyst and Families and Work Institute; New Study Shows Gender, Rank, and Regional Differences in Finding the Right Fit for Top Corporate Talent. May 21, 2008. https://familiesandwork.org/downloads/FindingFitforTopTalent.pdf

237. Kuhnert, K.W. & Lewis, P (1987). Transactional and Transformational Leadership: A Constructive/Developmental Analysis. Academy of Management Review. 1987, Vol. 12, No. 4.

238. Bill Gates, Founder of Microsoft. Source: http://www.dailymirror.lk/75949/bill-gate-s-transactional-leadership-style

239. US General Colin Powell (2015). Speech in Satterfield.

240. Weforum.org (2019). Study Shows that Relationships Have the Biggest Effect on Health. Republished study from Knowledge@Wharton, the online research ad business analysis journal of the Wharton School of the University of Pennsylvania. 01 Oct 2019. Source: https://www.weforum.org/agenda/2019/10/according-doctor-biggest-contributor-health/

241. Ghoshal, Sumantra (2015). 4 Secrets Of Strong Organizational Culture – "Smell Of The Workplace". Source: https://www.linkedin.com/pulse/smell-workplace-creating-right-context-success-sourabh-soni/

242. Virtues defined by Lao Tzu, described by Dr Wayne W. Dyer (2007). Change Your Thoughts—Change Your Life: Living the Wisdom of the Tao. Hay House; UK ed. edition

243. Selye, H. (1956). The Stress of Life. New York: McGraw-Hill.

244. Lazarus, R.S. (1966). Psychological Stress and the Coping Process. New York: McGraw-Hill.

245. Rampe, M. (2010). Der R-Faktor. Hamburg & Norderstedt: Books on Demand GmbH.

246. Orem, T. R., et al. (2019). Amygdala and prefrontal cortex activity varies with individual differences in the emotional response to psychosocial stress. Behavioral Neuroscience, 133(2), 203–211.

Acknowledgements

Our passion for leadership stems from having had the privilege of working with many great leaders and the privilege of sharing the concept of transformational leadership with employees, clients and students alike. We are honoured to work with those who also want to make a difference. Thank you to all of you as you have inspired us to write this book.

Specifically, we thank Peer Schatz for his contributions and foreword in this book. His willingness to challenge us and his ability to make sense of complexity, provide new perspectives and guide positive outcomes have ensured that we keep learning and growing, both personally and professionally.

To Thomas Schweins, Senior Vice President at QIAGEN, we have to say, "thanks boss, you are a truly transformational inspiration". Many others have also generously shared their time, including Natacha Piekatz-Hausammann, Rose Grayson and Sophie Grayson. We are extremely grateful for all their support.

We also thank Alison Staley for all her examples of transformational leadership in practice, and for being a sounding board for ideas and inputs. As an HR Consultant and Chartered Fellow of Chartered Institute of Personnel and Development, Alison has not only guided leaders, but has led large teams herself and knows the challenges and rewards of people management.

To our champions at OPTIMA, Joachim Dittrich and Heiko Kühne, a big thank you for believing in transformational leadership and sharing your practical examples from your own implementation.

To our proof-readers Emma Caldwell and Patrick Wilcoxson, we extend a massive thank you for your time and diligence to review our message, our flow and our spelling! It is your inputs that enable us to share our concepts in a way that others can also enjoy them more.

Index of Key Terms

CPSIA information can be obtained
at www.ICGtesting.com
Printed in the USA
BVHW050922071220
595089BV00005B/518

9 789464 075403